ALEXANDER THE GREAT

Casemate Short History

ALEXANDER THE GREAT

CONQUEROR, COMMANDER, KING

John Sadler and Rosie Serdiville

CASEMATE

Oxford & Philadelphia

Published in Great Britain and
the United States of America in 2018 by
CASEMATE PUBLISHERS
The Old Music Hall, 106–108 Cowley Road, Oxford OX4 1JE, UK
1950 Lawrence Road, Havertown, PA 19083, USA

© Casemate Publishers 2018

Paperback Edition: ISBN 978-1-61200-681-9
Digital Edition: ISBN 978-1-61200-682-6 (epub)

A CIP record for this book is available from the British Library

Printed in the Czech Republic by FINIDR, s.r.o.

Typeset in India by Versatile PreMedia Services. www.versatilepremedia.com

For a complete list of Casemate titles, please contact:

CASEMATE PUBLISHERS (UK)
Telephone (01865) 241249
Email: casemate-uk@casematepublishers.co.uk
www.casematepublishers.co.uk

CASEMATE PUBLISHERS (US)
Telephone (610) 853-9131
Fax (610) 853-9146
Email: casemate@casematepublishers.com
www.casematepublishers.com

CONTENTS

*In my opinion, at least, the splendid achievements of Alexander
are the clearest possible proof that neither strength of body,
nor noble blood, nor success in war even greater than
Alexander's own ... that none of these things,
I say, can make a man happy, unless he can win one
more victory in addition to those the world thinks
so great – the victory over himself.*

Arrian

For Gerry and for Ruth who make the writing possible.

INTRODUCTION

We few, we happy few, we band of brothers;
For he to-day that sheds his blood with me
Shall be my brother; be he ne'er so vile,
This day shall gentle his condition:

Shakespeare: *Henry V* Act 4: III

Thalatta, Thalatta! The Sea, the Sea – Xenophon's exclamation comes from the lips of a group of exhausted Greek mercenaries, who have for months fought their way out of the inland fastnesses of the Persian Empire to the Black Sea. It meant the world had changed. This band, a mere 10,000 strong, had marched clear across the Persian Empire in 401 BC and the mighty lords of the whole of the east had not been able to prevent them. Eighty years before, the legendary Three Hundred stood against Xerxes' (probable) hundred thousand and killed large numbers of them. The Athenians destroyed the invasion fleet and, next year, 30,000 Spartans and allies had wiped out the survivors at Plataea.

Shakespeare says, of Agincourt sixteen hundred years later, 'this story *shall the good man teach* his son; and Crispin Crispian *shall* ne'er go by from this day to the ending of the world, But we in it *shall* be remember'd'. It's cracking stuff. Aristotle might have said the same as he taught a rapt and eager Alexander all about the march of the ten thousand.

Most boys would love the stories and retell them to their sons. But Alexander, heir to the parvenu Philip of Macedon decided to do more; he decided to become even more famous by conquering

Alexander the Great. (Carole Raddato, Wikimedia Commons, CC-BY-SA 2.0)

the vast Persian Empire. He succeeded; nobody before or since, except perhaps Genghis Khan and Hitler, has ever come close.

Julius Caesar, one who was completely in thrall to the Alexander legend, is said to have wept when, at forty, he looked on his hero's statue and reflected on how weak his own achievement was by comparison. Ceasar was already eight years older than the Macedonian had been when he died.

Alexander was perhaps the greatest conquering general in history. In just over a generation, his northern Greek state of Macedon rose to control the whole nation. These uncouth northerners, seen by their neighbours as nouveaux-virtual barbarians would dominate the fissiparous polity of late classical Greece, a situation deeply resented by ancient city states such as Athens and Thebes. It was Alexander's father, Philip, who made this happen. It was his legacy that launched his son on a spectacular career of conquest, unequalled in history, that planted Hellenic culture across most of Asia. In a dozen years Alexander had destroyed the once mighty

Persian Empire, taken Egypt and the whole of Asia Minor, then pushed his army eastwards as far as the Indus. There had been nothing in history to quite equal this.

Flavius Josephus – Jewish fanatic turned Roman gentleman – wrote that the *Book of Daniel* had anticipated the arrival of Alexander in Jerusalem when it referred to 'the mighty Greek king who would conquer the Persian Empire'.[1] Conquer the Persian Empire he did, a stupendous feat of arms. Not since his hero Achilles had there been such a perfect warrior general. Plutarch describes him:

> The outward appearance of Alexander is best represented by the statues of him which Lysippus made, and it was by this artist alone that Alexander himself thought it fit that he should be modeled. For those peculiarities which many of his successors and friends afterwards tried to imitate, namely, the poise of the neck, which was bent slightly to the left, and the melting glance of his eyes, this artist has accurately observed. Apelles, however, in painting him as wielder of the thunder-bolt, did not reproduce his complexion, but made it too dark and swarthy. Whereas he was of a fair colour, as they say, and his fairness passed into ruddiness on his breast particularly, and in his face. Moreover, that a very pleasant odour exhaled from his skin and that there was a fragrance about his mouth and all his flesh, so that his garments were filled with it, this we have read in the Memoirs of Aristoxenus. (Plutarch: 4)

Peter Morris Green, a British historian who has analysed the statues and literary description, paints a not altogether flattering portrait:

> Physically, Alexander was not prepossessing. Even by Macedonian standards he was very short, though stocky and tough. His beard was scanty, and he stood out against his hirsute Macedonian barons by going clean-shaven. His neck was in some way twisted, so that he appeared to be gazing upward at an angle. His eyes (one blue, one brown) revealed a dewy, feminine quality. He had a high complexion and a harsh voice.[2]

---

1 *Jewish Antiquities* XI 337, viii 5.
2 From Peter Morris Green's *Alexander the Great* (London; Weidenfeld & Nicolson 1970).

Statue of Alexander in modern Macedonia. (Courtesy of Creative Commons CCO)

Alexander's **smell** is mentioned often, sweet breath and a clean, fragrant odour:

> The cause of this may have been the blend of hot and dry elements which were combined in his constitution, for fragrance if we are to believe Theophrastus[3] is generated by the action of heat upon moist humours. That is why the hottest and driest regions of the earth produce the finest and most numerous spices, for the sun draws upon the moisture which abounds in vegetable bodies and causes them to decay. In Alexander's case it was this same warmth of temperament which made him fond of drinking and also prone to outbursts of choleric rage. (Plutarch: 4)

This wouldn't have done at all at the time, Achilles could not be anything other than physically imposing, he had a heroic mould to fit. Alexander always had to try that bit harder. Achilles had

---

3 Theophrastus was a Greek philosopher and pupil of Aristotle.

the inestimable advantage of being mythical and did not have to contend with contemporary biographers. Alexander spent his life measuring himself against the myth of his hero and the reality of his father. He used the classical sculptor Lysippos as his principal artist, a sound choice. Lysippos is still regarded as one of the top three creative geniuses in his field in this era. His representations have long been regarded as accurate – though it is a wise artist who cleverly flatters his patron.

Alexander was famously close to his mother. Olympias was an immensely strong, domineering character, focused and totally ruthless. She was clearly a major influence as, undoubtedly, was his father despite their on/off, love/hate relationship. Philip was a successful conqueror in his own right – Alexander could not have wished for a more instructive military apprenticeship. One-eyed Philip, his former youthful beauty marred by many wounds, was a tough old warhorse. At the same time Alexander was in competition with the old man and both were prone to tantrums, usually lubricated by binge drinking.

Fame was the lure. If Achilles' blood, through his mother's line, ran in his veins then the quintessential Greek hero, another man devoted to his mother and astonishingly petulant, was his benchmark. Achilles was the greatest warrior of all. Not a pleasant role model to be sure – he is always portrayed as vain, arrogant, petty and conceited. But he was still the most famous of Greek heroes and that is what mattered to Alexander. His father had abundant ambition and the huge talent necessary to realise it. But Philip probably set limits to it. His whole life had been primarily a battle for survival – even his most aggressive strategies were essentially protectionist. His son accepted no limits; his ambition had no horizons. He went on and on, till his exhausted troops could go no further. His troops never stopped loving or revering him – he had just worn them out till they had nothing left. He was born to conquer and for nothing else. Had he not died young, history might have recalled him as a sad, mad, old dictator, a classical Stalin gazing malevolently from his pile of skulls.

Macedon was a pretty rough neighbourhood and political infighting, intrigue and murder were national pastimes. Alexander

Vase depicting Achilles tending Patroclus, c. *500 BC. (Bibi Saint-Pol, Wikimedia Commons)*

could be extremely, indeed utterly ruthless, frequently appearing vindictive – that was his cultural inheritance. He killed people to be sure but, mostly, they would have done the same to him or were actively about to. Much has been written about his sexuality. In fact, we have no real idea. Homosexuality was normal for his time and place: it carried no stigma. To be unmarried was more unusual and frowned on. A man must have an heir. Alexander married three times. His first alliance, to Roxanne was said to have been love at first sight. She bore him a son and, it was said, he had another by his alleged mistress Barsine. There is room for confusion here. His second wife, Stateira (a daughter of Darius II) was also referred to in antiquity as Barsine. There was a third spouse, Parysatis (daughter of Darius's predecessor, Ataxerxes III) who he married on the same day as Stateira. Nor were Alexander's the only nuptials that day.

Definitely Augustus visiting Alexander's tomb. (Sebastien Bourdon, Wikimedia Commons, US Public Domain)

The Susa weddings were a mass event arranged by Alexander in 324 BC in the Persian city of Susa. He wanted to symbolically unite the Persian and Greek cultures, by taking a Persian wife himself, celebrated with Persian ceremony along with his officers, for whom he also arranged marriages with noble Persian brides. The union was not only symbolic – their offspring would be the children of both civilisations.

These were political and dynastic moves aimed at cementing his position as Darius' legitimate successor. Why not, both were usurpers. Roxanne wasted no time in disposing of her rivals immediately after his death, eliminating not only personal rivals but a threat to her son: Stateira was said to be pregnant at the time of her death.

Alexander would be the benchmark against whom future empire builders would measure their success. He would become an emblem for muscular Christianity in Victoria's vast dominions: seen as one who had also taken the benefits of civilisation to brute nations

Alexander was surrounded by remarkable **women**, his grandmother Eurydice and mother Olympias were just two of them. His father was assassinated at the wedding of his full blood sister Cleopatra. Not the best start to married life but, in Macedon, pretty much par for the course. Cleopatra was marrying her maternal uncle Alexander of Olympias. She appears to have been a formidable young woman in her own right. When her husband died campaigning in north Italy, their son Neoptolemus succeeded, with his mother as regent. He did not come fully into his inheritance for thirty years – Cleopatra seems to have been a most effective ruler. When Alexander died, she became a highly eligible bride for one of his successors, scrabbling for chunks of empire. Like most of her line she died violently, though in uncertain circumstances around 308 BC, probably in her fifties.

who were secretly yearning for the opportunity and who should be grateful for it. Views have changed since of course. I doubt Alexander would have objected to this portrayal. Ultimately it was himself he was competing against, that would make him and finally destroy him. The life of Alexander the Great, like Macbeth, is a tragedy of ambition. Not because he failed but he succeeded so brilliantly.

All dates BC

371	The Thebans defeat Sparta at the battle of Leuctra. This marks the end of Spartan military hegemony.
368–365	Alexander's father Philip is a hostage in Thebes.
362	Epaminondas of Thebes is killed at the battle of Mantinea, decline of Theban power.
360–359	Following the defeat and death of Perdiccas III of Macedonia, Philip accedes to the throne.
359–358	Philip defeats the Illyrians.
357	Philip marries Olympias.
356	Birth of Alexander.
346	Alexander is educated until age sixteen by Aristotle.
338	Alexander fights his first battle against the armies of Athens and Thebes at Chaeronea, commanding the left of Philip's army.
337	Formation of the League of Corinth.
336	Alexander succeeds as Alexander III of Macedon when his father is assassinated. He disposes of any likely rivals.
336–335	Alexander fights the Illyrians, Thracians and Triballians before moving south against rebellious Thebes which he destroys.
334	He crosses the Hellespont to begin the conquest of Persia and wins the battle of the Granicus River.
333	Alexander cuts the Gordian knot and defeats Darius III at Issus.
332	Sieges of Tyre and Gaza.
332–331	He conquers Egypt and founds Alexandria.
331	Key battle at Gaugamela where Darius is defeated again, leading to the collapse and surrender of much of Persia.

330	Alexander takes and destroys Persepolis, Darius is murdered by his own side.
329–327	Confounding every general since, Alexander tries and largely succeeds in conquering what is today's Afghanistan. He marries Roxanne, daughter of Oxyartes.
327	Invasion of India.
326	Alexander defeats Porus at the battle of the Hydaspes but then faces a mutiny.
325	A tortuous return march from India.
324	Alexander reforms the army to integrate warriors from his empire.
323	Alexander the Great dies in Babylon.
316	Death of Olympias.
310	Assassination of Roxanne and Alexander's son Alexander IV.

WHO'S WHO?

Alexander III Alexander the Great

Alexander IV His son by Roxanne, murdered in 310 BC

Agis III King of Sparta, 21st ruler of the Eurypontid line

Antipater Macedonian general and father of King Cassander, Antipater was regent from 320–319 BC

Aristotle (384–322 BC) Greek philosopher and scientist, tutor to the young Alexander

Attalus A Macedonian general, father of Philip II's last wife Cleopatra Eurydice, killed by Alexander after his accession

Cleitus the Black A Macedonian general of ability, saved Alexander's life at the battle of the Granicus, later killed by him in a drunken brawl in 328 BC

Cleopatra Eurydice Daughter of Attalus and the last of Philip II's wives, killed by Olympias

Cleopatra of Macedon Alexander's sister, later Queen Regent of Epirus

Coenus An able Macedonian general, son in law of Parmenion

Craterus One of the *diadochi*, the rival generals who fought over Alexander's legacy, a venerable Macedonian officer

Darius III Ruler of the Persian empire

Demeratus A Corinthian but pro-Macedonian, liaised between father and son in the dispute between Philip and Alexander

Demosthenes Athenian statesman and orator

Diogenes (412–322 BC) Greek philosopher, known as 'the Cynic', said to have met with Alexander

Hephaestion Companion, probable lover of Alexander

Lysimachus of Acarnia Alexander's first tutor before Aristotle

Meleager A Macedonian officer, one who agreed the succession deal after Alexander's death, quickly got rid of by Perdiccas

Nearchus Macedonian naval commander and explorer

Olympias Alexander's mother, daughter of Neoptolemus I of Epirus, principal wife of Philip II

Oxyartes of Bactria Warlord and father of Roxanne, possibly one of the assassins of Darius III

Parmenion (c. 400–330 BC) Macedonian general who served Philip and Alexander. He was assassinated after his son Philotas was implicated in a regicidal conspiracy

Parysatis II A daughter of Darius III's predecessor, married to Alexander at Susa in 324 BC, probably subsequently murdered by Roxanne

Perdiccas Cavalry general and senior commander, took power after Alexander died, eventually assassinated by his own officers

Philip II Father of Alexander and founder of the Macedonian Empire in Greece

Philip III (Arrhidaeus) Alexander's half brother and nominal successor, but who lacked capacity

Philotas Son of Parmenion, executed after a supposed conspiracy

Porus Prince and native ruler of territories in what is now the Punjab

Ptolemy One of the diadochi who founded a dynasty which endured for three hundred years in Egypt

Roxanne Daughter of Oxyartes, wife of Alexander who bore him a son born c. 340 BC and died from poisoning in 310 BC

Stateira II A daughter of Darius III, married to Alexander in 324 BC, murdered by Roxanne

Spitamenes (370–328 BC) Leader of a rising in Sogdiana and Bactria

GLOSSARY

Agama A guard unit, exact composition uncertain.

Antilabe Handgrip of the hoplite shield, the *hoplon*.

Archihypaspists Brigade commander who led 3,000 hypaspists.

Chiliarch Battalion commander.

Dekades A 10-man squad, latterly increased to 16.

Diadochus (plural *diadochi*) Successor to Alexander, taking a portion of his empire.

Dora A shorter thrusting spear that was carried by hoplites.

Hetairoi Companion cavalry.

Hoplite A heavily armed Greek infantryman/civilian soldier of the classical era.

Hypaspist A 'shield bearer', man-at-arms or squire, essentially elite infantry, possibly more heavily armoured than the phalangites in the traditional hoplite manner, sometimes referred to as *argyraspides* or 'silver shields', a term not in use before the battle of Gaugamela in 331 BC.

Hypaspistai basilikoi Hypaspists of noble descent, effectively an officer corps.

Ilie (plural *ilai*) A cavalry squadron.

Kopis A curved slashing sword used primarily by cavalry, not unlike a longer version of a current Gurkha kukri.

Lochos (plural *lochoi*) A unit of sixteen *dekades*, commanded by a *lochnagos*. 256 men and four *lochoi* formed a *chiliarchy* and six made up a *taxis* of 1,500 soldiers.

Peltast	Elite light infantry.
Pezhetairoi	Foot companions.
Phalanx	The phalanx consisted of a line-up of several infantry units called *syntagmata* (or earlier the *lochos*), each of its 16 files (*lochoi*) numbering 16 men, for a total of 256 in each *lochos*. Each *syntagma* was commanded by a *syntagmatarch*, who together with his subordinate officers would form the first row of each block.
Pelte	A smaller shield than the *hoplon,* of a type carried by phalangites.
Phalangite	An individual soldier within the phalanx.
Prodromoi/sarissophroi	Light horsemen, scouts and skirmishers.
Proskynesis	Ritual abasement/prostration.
Sarissa	A form of pike.
Synaspismos	Effectively a shield wall.
Syntagma/speira	A strong double-company-sized formation of 256 phalangites, deployed in files 16 or 18 deep with ranks of 32 or 16.
Taxis	Brigade.
Telamon	Shield, smaller and less convex than the larger *hoplon* carried by the elite guard of the hypaspists.
Xiphos	A double-edged thrusting sword with a broad leaf-shaped blade, could be used for the cut or lunge.
Xyston	The cavalry lance.

CHAPTER 1

THE PRODIGY

It is my belief that there was in those days no nation,
no city, no single individual beyond the reach of Alexander's
name; never in all the world was there another like him,
and therefore I cannot but feel that some power more than
human was concerned in his birth …

Arrian: 7

On a fine autumn day in October 336 BC, Philip II of Macedon appeared a happy man. Why not, he was attending the important dynastic union of his daughter Cleopatra to King Alexander I of Epirus. It was a good match. The bride was his daughter by his dominant fourth wife Olympias, mother of his son Alexander. Olympias was herself an Epirote princess. The king was only recently reconciled to his formidable spouse and their son. Philip had taken another wife (Macedonian royalty was polygamous). This was another Cleopatra, daughter/niece (we are not sure which) of his general Attalus. Philip, besotted by the younger model had dubbed her Cleopatra Eurydice (Eurydice translates roughly as 'she whose justice spreads widely'). The young woman's ambitious braggadocio uncle had visions of a new dynastic succession, making an enemy of Alexander's mother. Olympias made a very dangerous opponent: she was not about to let any upstart princeling get in the way of her boy's inheritance.

Statuette of a dancing woman, 4th century BC. (Hiart, Wikimedia Commons, CC0)

By and large, Macedonian women's expectations were domestic, rather than political. It was a behind the scenes role, running the household, demonstrating female skills and looking after their children. Marriage was a social transaction aimed at creating relationships between families and the bride was seen as a valuable commodity. The wife of the king was mistress of his household and responsible for managing his residence and attending to the hospitality of guests. She might sometimes be present at the drinking parties for the men but mostly spent time in the women's quarters (*gynaikonites*) spinning and weaving in the company of the other women.

Intellectual pursuits were exceptional and girls were not generally schooled. Lower-status women enjoyed greater independence, frequenting the marketplace (agora) – some worked as midwives and nursemaids. The only truly independent women were the courtesans

(*Hetairai*). They circulated freely, attended symposia, entertained whomsoever they pleased and managed their own property.

However, royal women also played an important role in state affairs. Olympias was not alone in becoming actively involved in affairs of state. When Alexander was away in Asia, she represented the Macedonian state. After Alexander's death she issued decrees on behalf of the joint-kings and herself as well as 'in the name of the house of Philip and his son Alexander'.

Alexander's half sister, Thessalonike was born about 345 BC, the daughter of king Philip II by his Thessalian wife, Nikesipolis. Her birth fell on the same day that the armies of Macedon and the Thessalian league defeated the Phocians. Philip is said to have proclaimed 'Let her be called victory ('nike') in Thessaly'.

Thessalonike bore Kassandros three sons – Philip, Antipater and Alexander. After their father's death, she held a position of some influence: so much so that her son Antipater, angered at the favour shown to the youngest brother, murdered her.

Adeia Eurydike was married to Philip Arrhidaeus, Alexander's half brother. She was the granddaughter of two kings, Philip II and his brother, Perdiccas III. Her mother, Kynane, was the offspring of one of Philip II's war-brides, who was the daughter of Bardylis, an Illyrian warrior-chieftain Philip had defeated. Kynane was married to one of Philip's brothers, Amyntas, who was later executed on the charge of treason after Philip's assassination. At the age of eighteen this feisty young warrior woman led a civil war in her attempt to claim the throne. She was often mistaken for a boy and became quite a rabble-rouser among the foot-soldiers who admired her.

Roxanne was another figure who exercised influence beyond that expected of her gender. Daughter of a warlike people she grew up helping her brothers load arrows on the walls of her father's mountain outpost on the Soghdian Rock. Legendarily fierce-tempered, it is not hard to surmise that part of her attraction for Alexander might have been the degree to which she reminded him of his mother. She followed Alexander to India where she gave birth to a child who died soon after. She was pregnant again at the time of Alexander's death as was, it is said, the second wife, Stateira. Sisterly solidarity did not make any appearance there, indeed it may well have been Stateira's condition that motivated her poisoning by Roxanne.

Unlike most of the other Persian noblewomen who were quickly swept from sight after the Macedonians repudiated the marriages that had been arranged for them by Alexander, Roxanne managed to survive, but she and her newborn son were never truly accepted. The child, Alexander IV, born a month after Alexander's death, was of Soghdian blood, not a true-born Macedonian.

Roxanne's life after Alexander's death was not an easy one. Despised by most of the generals and known for her angry outbursts, she was isolated, dependant on Olympias. One can only speculate on the relationship between two such feisty women. Roxanne's life became a struggle as she tried to survive the maelstrom of Macedonian politics and intrigues of the Macedonian court. She could trace her bloodlines to an Assyrian queen and was used to a rich, indulged lifestyle, known for her temper, selfishness and arrogance. Alexander's generals considered her a mere campaign wife.

By contrast Persian women, both royal and non-royal, had a degree of independence which allowed them to exercise economic independence and gave them a place in society. Although it was a prosperous and impressive civilisation, many of its documents and records were destroyed during years of conquests and war, leaving only a few Greek sources to learn from. The Greek view of these women has come down to us – they often referred to Persian women as conniving or manipulative figures who took advantage of weak kings. But there is an alternative source. The Persepolis Fortification Tablets were found in the ruins of Persepolis. They are administrative records that tell us much about the day-to-day running of an empire and they give us a very different take on women's lives.

In general, we can say that Persian women enjoyed power, influence, and economic opportunities. They were involved in the military and owned businesses, and held the same jobs as men. Some women never married or had children, but this was not seen as a problem. Of course, Ancient Persian society was still patriarchal, and for the most part, men held higher positions than women. Women's status may have owed its perception to Zoroastrianism

– the dominant religion. Unusually for its time, it held men and women to be equals.

Of course, not all women enjoyed the same status or power in Ancient Persia. Royal women certainly enjoyed more influence than non-royal women. In art, we can see royal women depicted almost identically to men with similar clothes, hairstyles and poses.

The closer to the king they were, the higher the status. The king's mother's role in establishing royal lineage made her a particularly influential figure (the Persians may well have practiced consanguineous marriage, an ancient Achaemenid tradition). She may have been the daughter of King Artaxerxes II Memnon, or possibly of his brother Ostanes. If the latter, she married her own brother Arsames.

Sisygambis, the mother of Darius, seems to have been a particularly formidable figure. We are told that she became devoted to Alexander after her capture at Issus and that Alexander referred to her as 'mother'. That may have been rather more than mutual affection – the term 'mother' has a political tinge to it.

When Alexander and Hephaestion went together to visit the captured Persian royal family, Sisygambis knelt to Hephaestion to plead for their lives, mistaking him for Alexander – Hephaestion was the taller, and both young men were similarly dressed. When she realised her mistake, she was acutely embarrassed, but Alexander reassured her; 'You were not mistaken, Mother; this man too is Alexander'.

When the Persian army's Scythian cavalry broke through Alexander's forces to reach them during the battle of Gaugamela, she allegedly refused to celebrate what appeared at first to be Persian victory. Quintus Curtius Rufus informs us that Sisygambis could never forgive her son Darius for abandoning his family at Issus. After Darius was killed shortly following his defeat at Gaugamela, Alexander sent his body to her for burial. Called upon to mourn his death, she was reported to have said, 'I have only one son [Alexander] and he is king of all Persia'.

On hearing of Alexander's death, Sisygambis had herself sealed into her rooms and refused to eat. She is said to have died of grief and starvation four days later.

Statue of Philip of Macedon. (Gunnar Bach Pedersen, Wikimedia Commons, CC-PD-Mark)

But that was all to come. Back in 336 BC, Philip, at the age of 46, had cause for contentment; the dynastic rift seemed patched over and he could look back on a lifetime of astonishing achievement. He had fought many battles and it showed. His youthful good looks were marred by the many scars of campaigning: lame, blinded in one eye, aging, the old bull was sagging but still very much in charge as he contemplated the marriage of his daughter Cleopatra to King Alexander I of Epirus. The marriage was celebrated in Aegae (modern Vergina), Macedon's ancient citadel. As part of the ceremony, the king went on foot into the theatre glad-handing, letting his VIP guests know their conqueror was still a man of the people.

He had only seven bodyguards in attendance. One of them, Pausanias of Orestis, suddenly produced a concealed weapon and fatally stabbed the king. Philip was dead pretty much before he hit the ground and the assassin took off at speed. He needed to move

In 1977 a Greek archaeologist, Manolis Andronikos, began digging the **royal graves** near Vergina and excitingly found that two of the four main tomb complexes were undisturbed. The grave goods in Tomb II were sumptuous and have been identified with Philip. The greaves had been altered to accommodate his misaligned tibia and the occupant's skull had suffered damage consistent with the king's facial wound. A team from Manchester University later carried out facial reconstruction so we can actually see Philip as he probably looked. Though the reconstructed face looks older than its years, disfigured by the loss an eye, the visage is still a compelling one: a man of great capacity, sure of his power.

fast as the rest of the close-protection team, recovering from the shock, were after him. He nearly made it. His fellow-conspirators were waiting at the city gate with fast horses and Pausanias was pretty quick on his feet. He might well have escaped had he not tripped over a vine root and gone sprawling. He never rose; the vengeful six were on him and hacked him to death.

Of course, the question asked by all was who put him up to it and why? Nobody is quite sure. Aristotle tersely suggested that Pausanias had been somehow insulted by Attalus' clique. Half a century later the historian Cleitarchus embroidered the tale, later picked up by Diodorus. The later story is pure soap opera. Philip was bisexual in this tale, Pausanias his lover. The older man had dumped him for another pretty young man, confusingly with the same name. Pausanias (the discarded lover) had taunted his replacement. Somehow, the victorious rival ended up dead. But the dead man had been a member of Attalus' affinity; the king's father in law would have his revenge. He invited Pausanias to a dinner, got him drunk and then had him gang-raped. Philip, despite knowing of the assault, did nothing. Perhaps he wanted to keep Attalus on side, especially as he was to have joint command of the force about to leave for the Hellespont. They were to establish a balcony and facilitate the great invasion of Persia. Policy outweighed old loyalties. Philip bought the jilted and much abused lover off by promoting him within the royal guard. Philip had misjudged his man: the hurt festered and Pausanias took his revenge.

Many maintained Pausanias did not have the wit to think all this out for himself nor plan an escape. Fingers were soon being pointed at Olympias and possibly at her son too. She had much to gain and certainly the necessary steel to see it through. One ancient writer (Justin in his *Epitome of Pompeius Trogus*) maintains that Olympias erected a burial mound to the assassin and had annual sacrifices made to Pausanias' spirit, hardly the response of a distraught wife. Internal politics in Macedon were ruthless and robust, the stuff of a Tarantino film. Regardless of suspicions, with Philip dead, his twenty-year-old son was now king.

Alexander, according to Herodotus, could and did claim Hercules as an ancestor. The Argead dynasty traced their line from Temerus of Argus who claimed descent from the greatest of Greek heroes. Zeus himself featured as an ancestor in some versions. Much of the historical reality of the northern kingdom is shrouded in obscurity but it seems likely the dynasty was established by the mid-7th century BC and centred on Aegae. The first king we really know anything about is Amyntas I (*c.* 547–498 BC). His successor Alexander I sided with the Persians at Plataea which clearly did not help his Hellenic credentials. Xerxes even used him as an ambassador after the debacle at Salamis but he seems to have made up with the Greek allies after the final Persian defeat.

Macedon was really two distinct regions, upper and lower. The kingdom sprang up on the fertile plain north of Mount Olympus defined by the Halliacmon and Axius rivers. The infant kingdom began to swell north and west onto the higher hills of Upper Macedon absorbing a whole network of tribal lands, bounded by Thrace to the north-east and, west of them, the fractious Illyrians (with whom the Macedonians frequently scrapped). South was Thessaly, culturally similar, and west was Epirus: both of them were allies against the Illyrians. Around the year 512 BC Darius I sent representatives to Macedon following his infiltration into the Balkans. The 'Great King' demanded submission and Amyntas, who had little choice, bent his knee.

Decades of Persian control and influence followed. Macedon did well out of the alliance: it was left to enjoy near autonomy and the treaty was sealed with a marriage contract. Despite ultimately having backed the wrong side, Alexander I (*c.* 495–454 BC) managed to get himself welcomed back into the Hellenic sphere. Herodotus thought he might have been an ally of the Greeks all along: that he just conned Xerxes into thinking he was on team Achaemenid (the empire begun by Cyrus the Great around 550 BC). Or he might just have been cleverly playing both sides; you can't blame him given the precarious location of his midget realm squashed between two heavyweights. Still, the Greeks called him a friend (Alexander *Philhellene*) so he must have been convincing. His realm would have fitted into the modern United States over 100 times.

His successor Perdiccas II had greater difficulty maintaining the goodwill of the Hellenic city states – sparring with the Athenians, the Thracians and fissiparous rivals in Upper Macedonia. Athens found the coastal regions of Chalcidice compellingly useful as a source of raw materials and saw them as suitable for colonisation, prising settlements from beleaguered Perdiccas. The king fought back with four separate wars erupting till the onset of the Peloponnesian War which provided opportunities for alliances with Corinth and Sparta. Unsurprisingly, his initial approaches received a lukewarm response. He did finally make a treaty with Sparta but the relationship foundered and he switched to the Athenian side. Later on he reversed the switch, only one step above being a pawn in the fight between the big two. This move didn't prosper either so he swapped back to Athens. Macedon was not really anyone's idea of a desirable ally at this stage.

Perdiccas' successor Archelaus I managed to keep the peace with Athens and was able to build up his kingdom's resources, moving his capital to Pella. He gets credit for instigating a series of military reforms which would provide Philip II with the basic building blocks he would shape into a world-class fighting force. Archelaus was eventually assassinated, the victim of personal rivalries within the court. A rather scrappy interregnum followed with each usurper doing in his predecessor till in around 393 BC Amyntas III was last man standing.

After a troubled reign of over twenty years he was succeeded by his son Alexander II. It was he who, to secure an alliance with

Thebes, handed over his brother Philip as a noble hostage. Alexander's brother-in-law Ptolemy murdered him and set himself up as regent for the young Perdiccas III. By 365 BC Perdiccas was old enough to assassinate Ptolemy. He brought Philip back to Macedon and managed to achieve a measure of stability before he and his army were cut up by the Illyrians. Philip, by default, and again as last man standing, became king (although nominally only as regent for his nephew) in 359 BC. Nobody would have given much for his chances.

He had to move fast: Perdiccas had weakened the kingdom and enemies were coming in through the windows, Thracians from the east and Athenians from the coast. Philip bought off the Thracians and fought the Athenians. In three desperate and frantic years he turned the whole sorry show around. The respite gave him time to shore up internal resources and rebuild an army. Though he was now married to a great-grand-daughter of the Illyrian king, he set about avenging Perdiccas III. The Illyrians were utterly crushed, the slaughter this time round even greater. He took the added precaution of murdering his half brother Archelaus. Here was a new and dynamic player on the scene. Philip allied with Athens in a mutual pact but ratted on the deal and fought them alongside the Chalcidian League (Chalcidia had broken away from the Delian League during the Peloponnesian War and formed a separate bloc).

Brute force, selective killing, bribery and diplomacy were boosted by useful marriage alliances. Philip first married Phila, a young noblewoman of Upper Macedonia and followed up with his second marriage to Audata of Illyria before adding another brace of eligibles from leading Greek families. In 357 BC Philip married Olympias and Alexander was born a year later, the very time his father's horse passed the post first at the Olympic Games, clearly a good omen. It was said to have been a love match and the birth of an heir must have confirmed the relationship.

Two of his first wives had both died without leaving him a viable heir so Philip must have been worried. He had journeyed to Samothrace to be initiated into the fertility-linked mysteries and there he encountered Olympias. Dreams and portents were said to have followed. On the eve of her wedding Olympias apparently dreamed her womb was struck by lightning, sparking a great sheet

Olympias

Alexander's mother did not get a very good write-up from early commentators. That may reflect Roman-age writers – including Greeks like Plutarch, a native of Chaeronea. Lucius Plutarchus was a serious gossip, today he would be a sure-fire hit with the tabloids. His view of the queen reflects a contemporary suspicion of ambitious women. Macedon was essentially a male-dominated society but one where powerful women could play a role. Palace politics were robust – as many women died nastily as did their men. Olympias herself, her daughter Cleopatra, daughter-in-law Roxanne and both Alexander's Persian consorts died violently. Whether Olympias was the 'fiend-like' queen, '... a woman of a jealous and vindictive temper', or just a woman doing her best for her boy in highly risky circumstances is not clear. She certainly killed Philip's other younger widow and child but that was par for the course: the way things were done in Macedon. Her son remained devoted to her all his life and she took up the cudgels on behalf of her daughter-in-law and grandson (both later killed).

of consuming fire. Philip subsequently had dreams over the state of his wife's womb which portended something special would emerge from it. Those same portents may well have contributed to the cooling of their passion. It was said Philip had had another dream where he saw a serpent coiled up beside his sleeping consort. It is possible Olympias was a member of a Dionysian cult which involved wild sexual goings on in trance like states of ecstasy. That might have been an alarming prospect for a man like Philip: desperate to demonstrate that his heir was really the product of his loins.

Alexander was born healthy on the same day as the Temple of Artemis at Ephesus burnt down. Inevitably, there were soothsayers ready to insist this portended a great calamity befalling the east. They weren't wrong: 'At that moment Philip had just captured the city of Potidea, and he received three messages on the same day. The first was that his general Parmenion had overcome the Illyrians in a great battle, the second that his race horse had won a victory in

the Olympic Games, and the third that Alexander had been born'
(Plutarch: 3).

From an early age Alexander showed himself to be both strong-
willed and impulsive. Given his parentage that is hardly surprising.
He was clearly intelligent and articulate and he voiced his objective
early: fame and glory were to be his. Like his hero Achilles he was
close to his mother; her plans for him matched his own. There
were other children in the palace (besides Alexander and his sister
Cleopatra). Indeed, one was older, his half brother Arrhidaeus (born
to one of Philip's Greek wives). Arrhidaeus had severe learning
difficulties and ironically, that probably saved his life.

At the outset Alexander seemed to get on with his father too.
Philip recognised the boy had talent and ensured he got a good
education. Plutarch tells us that when his father was absent, the
boy took it upon himself to receive Persian delegates and chatted
amiably at length, keen to know of their travels. If they'd known
what this dialogue would lead to the Persians might have kept their
mouths firmly shut. Olympias' relative Leonidas took on the role of
mentor and hired Lysimachus as tutor. Then came the famous tale
of Bucephalus; a brave, clever boy tames the wild stallion everyone
else is afraid of, the horse that would carry its master half way round
the known world.

His father had cause to be impressed: 'Philip had noticed that his
son was self-willed, and that while it was very difficult to influence
him by force, he could easily be guided towards his duty by an
appeal to reason, and he therefore made a point of trying to persuade
the boy rather than giving him orders. Besides this he considered
that the task of training and educating his son was too important
to be entrusted to the ordinary run of teachers of poetry, music
and general education ... so he sent for Aristotle' (Plutarch: 7). To
persuade the great man to come north the king generously rebuilt
his home town of Stageira (which Philip had earlier wasted).

It was a sound appointment; the precocious boy met a man he
could respect and who would give him a world-class grounding – it
was a formidable learning partnership. Aristotle seems to have had
a genuine fondness for his brilliant and demanding student who
added a love of and knowledge about medicine to his portfolio.

Statue of Alexander and Bucephalus in Thessaloniki. (Nikolai Karaneschev, Wikimedia Commons, CC BY 3.0)

While the boy at times felt far closer to his teacher than his distant father, the relationship cooled as Alexander reached maturity and finally deepened into suspicion. The hero frequently exhibited traces of paranoia which became steadily more pronounced.

In the year Alexander was born another scrap, the Third 'Sacred' War flared up in central Greece between Phocis and Boeotia (Thebes being the capital of this region). One of the causes was an argument over who should control the Oracle of Apollo at Delphi (extant since prehistory). Thessaly was drawn into the brawl and the citizens of Larissa, his wife Philinna's home town, asked Philip for help against the Phocians. The latter were in alliance with the home city of one of his other wives – multiple marriages could lead to such embarrassments. He weighed in, saw off the Phocians and became effectively military governor of Thessaly. When he finally brought the war to an end the tamed Phocians were kicked off the prestigious board of the Delphic Amphictyony (or Delphic League. The League had started as a loose grouping designed to support and protect the Temple of Apollo at Delphi and that of Demeter near Thermopylae. By the 4th century BC, a series of disputes had erupted over who dominated the sites. Philip moved in. This wild outlander was set to rise.

As his son sat at the great man's feet, Philip, with astonishing speed, built up his hegemony in the Balkans. While he did suffer defeats, bite by bite his power grew and with territory came resources. He assumed sovereignty over most of the Greek settlements away from the Chalcidian Peninsula; capturing Crenides ensured a steady supply of gold and silver ore that would fund his wider expansion. He killed six thousand Phocians in the charmingly named battle of Crocus Field and captured half as many again. These prisoners he later had drowned. His cash funded a pro-Macedon faction in Athens and sponsored troubles which kept the Athenians distracted while he laid siege to the city of Olynthus – an important Chalcidian settlement (said to have been founded by Hercules' son). He took the place and flattened it. Others who defied him suffered the same fate.

Northern Greece was pretty much under his thumb. Mighty Athens and great Thebes were unable to compete; their influence over what was now the Macedonian sphere had all but vanished. This mattered. The city states had used the barbarous north as a source of raw materials and Athens remained heavily dependent on corn supplies coming in from the Black Sea region (probably what the Trojan War had really been about). Philip had turned north to fight the Scythians – nomadic peoples of Iranian origin and in 339 BC appeared before Byzantium. This could threaten Athens vital umbilical and also worried the Persians; control of the Hellespont mattered to everybody. Artaxerxes III sent money and men to Byzantium. His failure to take the city gave his enemies, simmering and resentful in Greece, enough backbone to have a go. They would wish they had not done so.

Philip had bought pro-Macedon factions in both Athens and Thebes. Artaxerxes now funded the opposition and drowned out Philip's chorus. Conversely, his friends in Thessaly wanted him to get more involved in Greece. Athens was backing the Byzantines: Philip riposted by grabbing their grain ships, striking at a major artery. The Athenians opted for war. Early in 339 BC Thebes had grabbed the important town of Nicaea which effectively blocked

Pella was Alexander's capital as well as his father's. The site has now been extensively excavated though it is not far from the grim, grime-coated, industrial suburbs of Thessaloniki. It was probably Alexander's ancestor Archelaus I who shifted his base here from the ancient heartland. Intending to dazzle, Archelaus invited artists and craftsmen to embellish his new palace, bling it up a bit to show the sneering Greeks to the south he had fully arrived. Euripides was an early and seemingly enthusiastic visitor. By Philip's day Pella, where he was born, was an established capital city and booming port – it was connected by a channel to the Thermaic Gulf. Most of the surviving fragments are post Alexander, dating from the time of his successors Cassander and later Antigonus when the city reached its peak. As Macedon declined its fortunes waned and it was sacked by Rome in 168 BC. It was later levelled by an earthquake.

The site was investigated by various gentlemen archaeologists in the 19th century and then dug properly by the Greek Archaeological Service in the late fifties. They uncovered the extensive agora and magnificent palace. It is huge, around 60,000 square metres, comprised of six to seven large groupings, rooms and structures all set out around a square courtyard. It was very much monumental, designed to dazzle, though the Greeks probably still sneered at the vulgarity.

the route south at Thermopylae. Philip had been drawn away from the failed siege by more bother at Delphi.

The citizens of Amphissa had begun cultivating land sacred to Apollo on the Crisaean plain south of Delphi. The Amphictyonic council decided to declare a sacred war against them, with forces led by Philip. This gave him the pretext to campaign in Greece.

Philip promptly cowed the Amphissans, then took the opportunity he had been waiting for. He kept going straight towards Athens and it took Demosthenes' most persuasive oratory to stem the resultant panic. The able Demosthenes was then sent off to Thebes to broker an alliance despite the cities' traditional mutual dislike. Philip made use of a long-forgotten route over Thermopylae to outflank them all, slipping into central Greece.

The reckoning with Athens and her new ally Thebes didn't occur till August the following year as it seemed Philip was trying diplomacy. If so it did not work. Even at this point Macedon and Thebes were not formally at war. A negotiated truce could have been brokered but the Thebans had thrown caution to the winds and their lot in with Athens. As it happened the Athenians, following their initial panic, had mobilised and would be able to join their new friends within days. This was serious. Philip was formidable and his track record impressive but he was still just a northern upstart as far as his enemies were concerned. This would be his most serious test to date. He did not fail.

Frustratingly, we don't know that much about the campaign. Philip had to get his army from Phocis into Boeotia which meant forcing one of the high passes. There were clearly some sharp skirmishes but it wasn't until mid-summer that he bulldozed his way through and came down the highway which the Greeks had blocked at Chaeronea. Diodorus gives Philip 30,000 infantry and 2,000 cavalry which he led personally. Alexander at eighteen must have got his first real taste of battle and of divisional command; leading the phalanx on the left. Not quite first blood, as Plutarch tells us Alexander, acting as teen regent for his father, had previously dealt with a revolt of the Maedi, a tribe from north-west Macedonia. Naturally, for this coming fight, the young man would be guided by a cadre of experienced senior officers.

We have no information on the exact size of the Greek forces but it's not improbable they were roughly equal perhaps even larger than the Macedonians. The bulk were provided by the main players; Thebes and Athens with detachments from Achaea, Corinth, Chalcis, Epidaurus, Megara and Troezen. Generals Chares and Lysicles commanded the men of Athens on the left, with their composite allies holding the centre and the Thebans under Theagenes to the right. Their choice of ground was sound; the army straddled the road, their left flank brushed up against higher ground rising towards Mount Thurion while the right flank was covered by the River Kephisos. Aware Philip's standard tactical gambit would be a blow against the Greek left, their line was echeloned, that is, slanted north-eastwards. If he barreled ahead into the Greeks he

Cavalryman with kopis – *or 'cleaver', curved slashing sword with protective handle. (By kind permission of John Conyard)*

would leave the flank of the infantry exposed at the vital hinge. Worse, the Greek left occupied higher ground. It was a very well-judged position and Philip of Macedon was facing premiership opposition.

Accounts of the fighting are limited and potentially suspect. What may have happened is that Philip sent the whole line forward, infantry to pin the enemy centre and right while he attempted to break the Athenians on the left with his cavalry. The first charge failed, the line was too strong and the ground unfavourable. Philip then fell back, the 'Parthian retreat', a ruse to draw the enemy on in some disorder. It's a tricky maneouvre, the strategy could easily have rebounded if Philip's men had lost their collective nerve and run for real. If that happened, there would have been no halting them. Philip succeeded; his men so well trained, that they turned and reformed and this time broke through. Meanwhile, or possibly beforehand, Alexander had used his companions as shock troops, bursting the Theban line. Historians have long been exercised as to whether these companions were in fact cavalry, his household men or some kind of elite infantry.

Did Philip deliberately prolong the opening phase to tire out the relatively raw Athenians, his own tough veterans being far more acclimatised to the sapping rigours of combat? This may be right: Diodorus does say the fight was long and costly to both sides, an effective deadlock. Current military historians certainly incline to this view. Philip did prolong the battle (or initially could get nowhere and after claimed it was all part of a cunning plan), but then he pivoted on the centre. This was the hinge between the heavy infantry of hoplites on the right, but left of the cavalry and the phalanx. So the right echeloned back, drawing the Athenians out while the left crashed into the Thebans. That avoided opening up any dangerous gap between the left- and right-hand corps.

As the Thebans buckled, the Athenians disordered advance left them exposed and Philip's prepared blow smashed them. At the same time Alexander on the left delivered his killer-punch against the Thebans. It is unclear whether Alexander's brigade was mounted or dismounted but they struck at the Theban praetorians, their Sacred Band, the band of lovers, as Mary Renault termed them. These had been placed on the extreme right of the Greek line as an anchor.

If Alexander had been mounted, his cavalry regardless of their élan, could not hack through a line of spears: '… And [Alexander] is said to have been the first to break the line of the Theban Sacred Band. Even in my own time an oak tree used to be pointed out near the river Kephisos which was known as Alexander's Oak, because his tent had been pitched beside it at that time, and not far away is the mass grave of the Macedonians who fell in the battle' (Plutarch: 9). The Theban elite battalion was effectively wiped out. This battle was over. Diodorus tells us that close to a thousand Athenians died and as many Thebans, many more were taken prisoner. How many Philip lost is unclear but his casualties will not have been light[1].

Greece now belonged to Philip of Macedon. Athens and Corinth feverishly prepared for siege. They need not have bothered, they had misread Philip. He did not intend to subjugate Greece; he needed

---

1 Plutarch suggests all three hundred of the Sacred Band died in the battle. They have or it is supposed they have, their own war memorial the 'Lion of Chaeronea'. Archaeology has revealed the remains of 254 young males beneath the stone lion which clearly caps a mass grave. These may well be the dead of the Sacred Band (probably not all died on the field or they may have been below their nominal muster as most units tended to be).

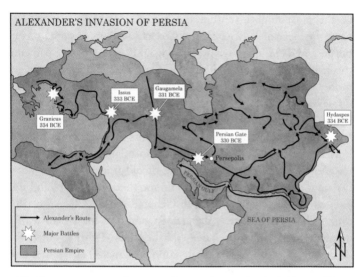

ALEXANDER'S INVASION OF PERSIA

Granicus 334 BCE

Issus 333 BCE

Gaugamela 331 BCE

Persian Gate 330 BCE

Persepolis

Hydaspes 334 BCE

PERSIAN GULF

SEA OF PERSIA

→ Alexander's Route

☆ Major Battles

▨ Persian Empire

N

The Persian empire at the time of Darius III, 336 BC. (Chloe Rodham)

the city states on side for a much bigger project – the invasion of Persia. He thought bigger than they did. In Thebes he kicked out his enemies and brought back his friends, creating what was, in effect, martial law. He fined the Thebans heavily; they had to ransom their prisoners and pay for the interment of their dead. He could have done much worse and the Thebans would have done well to reflect on this.

Next spring a major convention of all the Greek city states met at Corinth. What Philip wanted was their support against Persia. In part he was pushing on an open door, the Greeks had an ancient grudge to settle and, if Philip turned his attentions east, they were no longer in his sights. Only the Spartans demurred; as ever their xenophobia prevailed and they were accustomed to giving orders, not taking them. This was Philip's crowning ambition, to finally be the man who brought the great Achaemenid Empire to its knees. He would be the liberator of all those Greek colonies of Asia Minor which had been under the lash for so long.

This would be a massive undertaking, the greatest invasion in history since Xerxes had come the other way. It would certainly be the most mighty venture any had ever embarked upon. Not since the Siege of Troy would the Greeks have known such unity of purpose and the new Agamemnon would be the former parvenu, the half-wild northerner Philip of Macedon. You could not get more Greek than that. The Corinthian League was agreed and set up. It would take a year to organise the logistics but, in March 336 BC, veteran generals Parmenion and Philip's new father/uncle in law Attalus would take the vanguard across the Hellespont.

Meanwhile on a domestic front Philip might have been getting on and slowed up by his catalogue of old injuries but his other desires were unimpaired. There is no fool like an old fool and this one fell for the daughter/niece of General Attalus, Cleopatra. This time Philip was in love, a dangerous condition for a man with a domineering older wife and established heir. Polygamy had the advantage of ensuring a healthy supply of male heirs but it also frequently led to a surfeit of them. In Macedon this was often resolved by murder. While her husband's many amours need hardly trouble Olympias as queen, the arrival of a fertile younger version was cause for concern. Once you throw strong drink into the mix it becomes highly combustible.

Philip clearly did love his son and was inordinately proud of his achievement at Chaeronea, certainly not jealous of Alexander's laurels. But, 'Cleopatra's uncle Attalus, who had drunk too much at the banquet, called upon the Macedonians to pray to the gods that the union of Philip and Cleopatra might bring forth a legitimate heir to the throne …' (Plutarch: 9). What the fool meant was that Cleopatra was good Macedonian stock and Olympias an outlander.

Alexander, who presumably had not been teetotal, got very mad indeed; Attalus had effectively called his mother a barbarian whore and him a bastard. He threw his cup at Attalus, missed; Philip staggered to his feet and drew on his son before he fell over. Alexander could have left it at that but nobody ever does; 'here is the man who was making ready to cross from Europe to Asia, and who cannot even cross from one table to another …' (Plutarch: 9). Sobering up, Alexander fled the court taking Olympias with him. He deposited his mother in her native Epirus before choosing Illyria as his temporary bolt-hole.

Philip must have bitterly regretted the whole incident. There is no evidence he had any intention of siring another potential successor and equally there's no doubt he loved his boy. The elder son Arrhidaeus lacked capacity and was no threat. It took Philip's old friend Demaratus the Corinthian to act as honest broker and mend the rift and Alexander was persuaded to return. The relationship remained fraught, the old bull and the young one.

In the year of the king's death, Pixodarus, the governor or *satrap* of Caria (Western Anatolia), had a bright idea. He would form a union with the up and coming Macedonians by marrying his daughter to the older son. Now Olympias took this to mean Alexander was to be somehow outflanked by his older half brother even though he could never rule. Alexander, without reference to his father sent his own emissary back, suggesting he would be a far more suitable bridegroom. Philip was enraged and sacked four of his son's intimates as a lesson in humility. It didn't work.

Olympias wasted no time in taking her revenge on her upstart rival. Pausanias tells us that, not content with a clean kill, she had the unfortunate girl and her infant child barbecued. Attalus was one of the twin Macedonian commanders of the vanguard establishing the vital bridgehead into Asia so this was embarrassing. Alexander had him killed anyway, alleging treasonable correspondence with the Persians. Such are the perils of binge drinking.

CHAPTER 2

THE IRRESISTIBLE PHALANX

The smallest detail taken from an actual incident in war is more instructive to me, a soldier, than all the Thiers and Jominis in the world. They speak for the heads of state and armies, but they never show me what I wish to know – a battalion, company or even platoon in action. The man is the first weapon of battle. Let us study the soldier, for it is he who brings reality to it.

Ardant du Picq

Any conqueror is only ever as good as the army he leads. Alexander had the great advantage of inheriting a seasoned fighting machine from his father. Innovative as both father and son were, the phalanx was not their idea – it was a development of hoplite warfare. The Greek hoplite was the heavy infantryman of the classical age. He had stood at the Hot Gates of Thermopylae, at Plataea and through the long agony of the Peloponnesian War. He was a citizen, he belonged; usually a man of property who could afford his own weapons and gear.

His motivation was simple; he defended his homeland and his property. His image has endured, a bronze *Corinthian* style helmet with nodding horsehair crest, heavy bronze cuirass, padded arming type tunic underneath, shaped greaves to cover the calves, a convex *hoplon* shield, hefty fighting spear and back-up sword. The spear with a shaft 2–3 metres long was his principal weapon, used primarily for thrusting over-arm. His sword with a blade about

Amphora showing hoplites fighting c. *540 BC*

0.6 metres in length was leaf-shaped and intended for thrusting, not entirely unlike the later Roman *gladius.*

Bronze offers good protection but it is heavy. The stylish and suitably heroic 'muscle' cuirass began to give way to a more composite corselet made from linen or canvas, glued together to offer a flexible but robust defence. Metal scales added another protective layer. It was cylindrical, with two broad shoulder straps and its lower section layered or feathered (*pteruges*). This gear wrapped around the wearer's torso and was laced up the left-hand side where, in a contact, he'd be covered by his shield.

This shield, the famous *hoplon*, was a solid piece of kit, comprised of a timber core with bronze outer layer and leather inner. It was held by an arm loop and handle to give a solid grip, the vulnerable strip in front of the arm often reinforced. It was none too light either, weighing in at around 8 kilos. To be able to heft the equipment, march and then fight demanded high levels of physical fitness.

Infantry tended to dominate, Homer's bronze clad Achaeans had ridden in chariots but these were long gone and the broken, often mountainous terrain of Greece was less suited to cavalry.

Companion cavalryman. (By kind permission of John Conyard)

Macedonia, nonetheless, the uncouth northern neighbour, did have a long tradition of mounted warfare and Alexander's elite companions would be the cream of his army.

It is said it was the adoption of the heavy shield that gave rise to the phalanx (not that it was that new, Homer's heroes had fought this way). The warriors deployed in files (from front to rear as opposed to ranks which tell off across the line), generally if by no means exclusively eight deep. Distance was about 2–2.5 metres, a pretty loose formation. This was suitable for manoeuvre and permitted skirmishers to pass through easily enough. Just prior to engaging, the ranks tightened to give every man his metre of frontage, spear held in the right hand, shield on the left side covering his comrade.

Rear ranks could move up to replace casualties or add weight for a push. This reliance on shields for protection could cause a general slide to the right with unfortunate consequences. Officers led by example, even senior commanders (*strategoi*). Survival in the phalanx depended on training and morale, drill made a big difference. Once the unit was committed, generals could not necessarily do much to affect the outcome (other than by leading by example).

Students of the Wars of the Three Kingdoms might recognise something of the 'push of sarissa' in hoplite warfare reminiscent of a rugby scrum. Spear heads were often of inferior, soft steel and therefore not ideal for penetration. If you could not stab your opponent you just had to bulldoze him. Often, as was frequently the case in battles, he who gave ground and broke would suffer disproportionately heavy casualties; failure in the scrum often meant death as the victors surged through.

Greek hoplites beat the Persians at Marathon in 490 BC and again massively at Plataea eleven years later. Future aggression would be coming from west to east not the other way round. That said, the Greek city states did not always fare well on success. It fostered disunity and intercnine strife. From 478 BC to the outbreak of the disastrous civil war in 431, Athens enjoyed a cultural and political zenith, heading the defensive or Delian League. Moreover, in that half century Athens flourished as an artistic and creative force, one long claimed as a driver of Western culture. Further south the Peloponnesian League was headed by conservative Sparta, militarily superb but aesthetically stilted. Insular and oppressive, the Spartan regime was in many ways the antithesis of cosmopolitan outward-looking Athens. The inevitable clash, a generation of bitter and bloody war, resulted in the total eclipse of Athens, ruined and degraded by that long, terrible war.

Sparta failed to significantly prosper or gain from her victory. The state was bankrupt and her habitual harshness did little to commend the Lacedaemonians to their allies who were treated more like subjects. This was not to the liking of the more robust states such as Thebes and Corinth who were linked to an Athenian revival and challenged Sparta's hegemony. The Corinthian War (394–387/386 BC) ended with another Spartan victory facilitated, ironically, by Persian bribes. The Thebans were not done, however, and fresh conflict burst out in the decade which followed till, at the battle of Leuctra in 371 BC, the brilliant Theban general Epaminondas finally destroyed the myth of Spartan invincibility.

Now it was, if briefly, Thebes' turn to intermeddle in the lands to the north, Thessaly and Macedonia, semi-wild margins. Philip, Alexander's father, had been a hostage in Thebes where, as a youth he met the great Epaminondas. It was to be a precarious apprenticeship. His older full brother King Perdiccas III, was killed, along with four thousand Macedonians, fighting against the Illyrians. Young Philip was in a very insecure position, salvation took considerable diplomatic and military dexterity. Happily he possessed both in abundance and began developing the drills and skills of his available forces.

According to Quintus Curtius Rufus[1]:

> The Macedonian line is certainly coarse and inelegant but it protects behind its shields and lances immovable wedges of tough, densely packed soldiers; the Macedonians call it a phalanx, an infantry column that holds its ground, they stand man next to man, arms interlocked with arms. They wait eagerly for their commander's signal and they are trained to follow the standards and not break ranks. (3.2.13)

Macedon was not a wealthy country, an often mountainous region without large-scale commerce or external trade. Subsistence farming was frequently beset by endemic tribal feuds and raids. There were few towns and nothing to rival the magnificence of Athens or Thebes. Nonetheless, this hardy yeoman stock, not dissimilar perhaps to the early North Italian legionaries of Rome, made excellent recruits and there was no shortage of them. Being primarily herdsmen they were less tied by the seasons than their contemporaries further south. They were, for the most part, dirt poor and the lure of loot was a very considerable incentive. It needed to be for, at the outset, they were raised by conscription not contract.

Philip had to move fast, he had taken on a remote kingdom sandwiched between powerful and aggressive neighbours. The previous incumbent, his elder brother, had died in battle and the cream of his men had gone with him. He could and did buy in mercenaries but that cost money he did not have. At the end of the day, hired guns are no substitutes for patriots. Terms like patriotism or nationalism are not terms you can use of Macedon in the 4th century BC. The name was largely a geographical expression:

1 A 1st century AD Roman writer, author of *Histories of Alexander the Great*.

Hellenistic officer. (By kind permission of John Conyard)

people identified with family, tribe or a wider affinity. That is what Philip and, later, Alexander would change. These outlanders would march over 20,000 miles on campaign, pushing way beyond the boundaries of the Hellenic World, beyond even the great vastness of the Persian Empire. They would become the very breath of Greek culture and ideas. They came down from their high, bare pastures and changed the world.

Later on they would get their reward. One of the cashflow benefits of stripping Persia was that the empire was a great cash-cow. Her loot and resources funded her ruin and Alexander's onward march. The excellent roads and communications networks along Darius' extended highways meant supplies and reinforcements could be kept moving, mail services maintained and Alexander's staff could maintain the civil administration of the conquered territories. Discipline in the army appears to have been fierce; overall, control was absolute for officers and men alike, floggings may have been commonplace and executions far from rare.

Whatever the basic motivation of his soldiers, Alexander inspired loyalty. To them he was the new Achilles. Why not, he always led them to victory:

> The Macedonians have a natural tendency to venerate their royalty, but even taking that into account, the extent of their admiration, or their burning affection for this particular king is difficult to describe. First of all, they thought his every enterprise had divine aid. Fortune was with him at every turn and so even his rashness had produced glorious results … Then there are the things generally regarded as rather unimportant but which tend to find greater approval among soldiers: the fact he exercised with his men, that he made his appearance and dress little different from an ordinary citizen's, that he had the energy of a soldier. (Curtius Rufus: 3.6. 18–19)

At the start of his great campaign east of the Dardanelles, Alexander had only very limited resources: According to Aristobulus (*c.* 375–301 BC, a Greek historian who served as a military engineer on Alexander's campaigns): 'The money available for the army's supplies amounted to no more than seventy talents, Duris (*c.* 371–281 BC, Duris of Samos, a Greek historian) says that there were supplies for only thirty days, and Onesicritus (who accompanied Alexander as a sailor, probably a helmsman, not an admiral as he claimed) that Alexander was already two hundred talents in debt' (Plutarch: 15).

Their battle-winning weapon, the *sarissa*, was not new. What was new was the use Philip made of it and the way he trained his men how to wield it. Eighteen centuries later King James IV of Scotland tried to replicate the trick, beasting his traditional spear formations into great columns of pikes, a process Philip would have instantly recognised. James didn't have long enough nor did he possess that same genius for war. He nearly got the idea but not quite. It cost him and Scotland very dear. In the superb Shefton Collection[2] in

2 Professor Brian Shefton opened a small museum to house his classical collection within Newcastle University in 1956 where it remained until being incorporated within the Great North Museum in 2008.

There's been endless speculation on the **sexuality** of Alexander's men. That homosexual relationships existed is obvious, the elite of Thebes' army were the 150 male couples or 'Sacred Band', men united in physical as well as comradely bonds. Whilst this was a specific instance, such relationships were clearly both common and tolerated, perhaps even a near norm. Relationships between younger and older men were accepted: the mentoring role could spill over into a more physical bond. Greece was not the only society to show such tolerances. As late as the 19th century in India, the Raj was not entirely opposed to such relations between young officers, preferring single-sex encounters within the regiment as opposed to liaisons with bazaar women and the inevitable medical consequences.

Newcastle's Great North Museum is a perfectly preserved bronze butt pike for a sarissa. It's beautifully cast and high quality. Recent research into ancient battle wounds suggests the sharp, pike end could be used for a jabbing blow against a fallen opponent to finish him off.

For most of Alexander's reign, the *phalangites*, probably no more than 10,000 strong at any one time, were conscripted on a localised or regional basis, not quite the Pals' battalions of WWI perhaps but bound by local loyalties and affinities. Senior officers were drawn from regional gentry. This made sense. The men would be serving with people they knew and taking orders from those they were already accustomed to obey, an extension of the tribal type conflict they were inured to. What they got from Philip was a coherent national command structure, uniform equipment and training, lots of it. These upland herdsmen were already tough, they could cover ground and they were not shy of a fight. Their king burnished and worked on these core capacities to build a world class army.

It was no picnic this national service. Recruits could expect to undergo 30-mile route marches in full kit, carrying their own water and rations. Like the famed and much burdened Republican legionaries, 'Marius' Mules', they only had a single servant per squad. This was the 10-man *dekas* – soon increased to 16 – remarkably similar to the Roman *contuburnium*. A group who served, messed and slept together, a natural bonding, fostering trust and *esprit de corps*. Legionaries referred to each other as 'brother', possibly phalangites did so as well. Besides, practice makes perfect and the phalanx in full battle array, weapons and armour burnished to high gloss, stamping and chanting, swinging and moving like some huge, giant hedgehog, the lines of points intimidating in the extreme, would have been a terrifying sight. Victory is all about psychology, an over-awed enemy is as good as beaten.

In a potentially tight spot Alexander used drill as a tactic, 'shock and awe' to freak out an adversary before a blow was struck:

> Such being the situation Alexander drew up the main body of his infantry in mass formation 120 deep, posting on either wing 200 cavalrymen with instructions to make no noise, and to obey orders smartly. Then he gave the order for the heavy infantry first to erect their spears, and afterwards, at the word of command, to lower the massed points as if for attack, swinging them, again at the word of command, now to the right now to the left. The whole phalanx he then moved smartly forward and wheeling it this way and that caused it to execute various intricate movements. Having thus put his troops with great rapidity through a number of different formations, he ordered his left to form a wedge and advanced to the attack. (Arrian: 1.6)

Shaken, the enemy abandoned their forward positions and retreated smartly into their citadel.

What Philip developed (and Alexander maximised) was a first-rate fighting machine based on the company or *syntagma* of say 250 men. This comprised of 16 files (*lochoi*) each of 16 men, commanded by an officer called the *syntagmarch* who took station at the front on the right of the line, junior officers placed behind him, his second in command or *ouragos* stood at left rear. Each rank was led by an NCO or *lochagos*, half files by the *hemilochites*, quarters by an *enomotarch*. The files were headed, two by a *dilochites*, four by *tetrarchs*, eight a *taxiarch* with the senior man in charge of the lot. So the ratio of officers to men was quite

Phrygian helmet. (By kind permission of John Conyard)

high, essential to maintaining not just discipline but cohesion. Each unit had its own herald, trumpeter, signaller and adjutant or *extra-ouragos*.

There is no consensus as to the individual attributes of the phalangite and the *hypaspist*. Possibly the latter were more akin to a typical hoplite with a shorter fighting spear and heavier armour. It is just possible they equated to the swordsmen who guarded the flanks of the much, much later Swiss sarissa columns. They were elite. The perhaps more humble Macedonian sarissa-man would carry a lighter shield, secured with a neck strap. Wielding the heavy sarissa was a two-handed job – adding the additional weight of a full size *hoplon* shield just would not work. His body armour would be lighter, and he would not necessarily, unless he was an officer,

Horse archer. (By kind permission of John Conyard)

wear greaves and a Thracian-style helmet. The latter, also known as a Phrygian, possibly derives its shape from the native leather cap with the wearer's face less enclosed than with the earlier classical Corinthian style.

Within the Macedonian phalanx, like its hoplite forbear, open order gave each phalangite 1.8 metres square of space that was halved before contact. As the great bristling hedgehog stomped forward, the long points of the first five ranks projected like a steel-tipped avalanche. If the unit stood back on the defensive it 'locked' shields with a narrowed frontage but some depth (5.5 metres) deployed 'edge on' to the enemy. Their smaller shields were bunched on the man in front, providing a kind of movable fortress, a bulldozer that could stamp its way forward. Discipline was the key. Drill, drill and more drill, no doubt the ranks and files groused. They probably groused a lot, it is what soldiers do but they would know their lives literally depended on it.

Like the later Scottish schlitron the phalanx was a flexible formation. The companies could deploy in line, in echelon, as a wedge or crescent and form a square – equally as versatile in attack as in defence. That's where the level of discipline came in and the high ratio of officers and NCOs to ordinary ranks. Even if the leaders sustained casualties (leading from the front was always a risky business) there would be a sufficient officer cadre still on their feet to hold the show together and keep it moving.

Before Philip, the Macedonians had used horses, fast agile ponies, ideal for skirmishing and horse archery. The animals were quite small and, of course, stirrups and even cavalry saddles were some way in the future. By Alexander's day he and his father had revolutionised the use of cavalry to create a strike force of great tactical impact, a battle winning tool. The elite companion cavalry (*hetairoi*), were usually led by the king in person, with him taking command of his personal squadron (*ile*) of horse-guards. These were now shock troops not skirmishers, though these were still needed (*prodromoi*), always a vital role for the cavalry. Like Cromwell's Ironsides, they were well armed and armoured, trained to charge home for maximum impact.

All wore helmets, most likely of the Boeotian type which left the face open while giving protection to skull and neck – visibility was more important to a horseman. Heavy bronze cuirasses covered the torso while greaves protected vulnerable calves. Both the straight, leaf bladed sword and the curved sabre/cleaver were worn but the lance remained a principal weapon. Gorgeous as they might appear on review the cavalry were very much warriors for the working day, carrying most of their kit and supplies on the saddle.

In terms of formations, the cavalry generally deployed as a square, 16 horses wide and half that in depth, each rider having say 1.2 metres frontage. Light cavalry were more likely to shake out into a looser wedge or rhomboidal deployment. The squadron was normally made up of 200 riders with four such units forming a mounted regiment or *hipparchia*.

On the battlefield, the phalanx held the centre, irresistible in attack and resolute in defence. Despite the weight of their cumbersome weapons, the sarissas could deploy rapidly and with considerable flexibility. Alexander would station his cavalry, *en masse*, on the right of the line, poised to deliver a knockout blow.

Not all battles were fought in the field. Much of Alexander's time was spent on **sieges**. The phalanx was not much use there: hoplite infantry were better suited to storming an enemy's fixed defences. Much of the work of was the gruelling, exhausting and endlessly sapping business of siege lines. Alexander was to become a master, with an impressive range of artillery to deploy. The *gastraphetes* ('belly-bow') was a kind of early crossbow, tricky and slow to load so not much use in battle or in the open. With a draw-weight of 150–200 pounds (68–90 kg) it had great range and penetration. Moving up the scale, the *oxybeles* was a more powerful and frame-mounted weapon, using torsion and spanned by a winch. This had yet greater range and surprising accuracy as many a dead defender could have attested. These devices shot bolts whereas the larger *lithobolos* shot stones, from 4.6 kg up to an impressive 82 kg. As the siege progressed, these engines were brought in as close as possible – 150–200 metres – so that their shot could damage masonry and shatter merlons as well as keeping defenders' heads down.

At the articulated joint in the line he would place the hoplite armed hypaspists between the sarissas and horses, to give that greater cohesion. Not being weighed down with heavy sarissas and, as an elite force of heavy infantry, the hypaspists could exploit success or reinforce danger as circumstances dictated.

After trashing Darius at the battle of Issus in 333 BC Alexander marched south along the Levant coast. He needed to secure the great coastal cities to prevent Persian ships outflanking him and attacking Greece. Both Sidon and Byblos got the message and opened their gates. Tyre proved less amenable. The city would not resist overtly but was not going to simply open her gates to the invader. The citizens had some reason for confidence: their city was constructed offshore and they had plenty of ships, rather more than Alexander, so a naval blockade was not going to work. Any assault would have to come from the landward side and the Macedonian sappers, who certainly knew their trade, began to throw out an extended causeway.

The further they went, the harder and deeper it got and the closer they came within range of the defenders' artillery. Alexander added two strong towers to the further, seaward end of his approach and filled these with a repertoire of machines that could provide cover and counter-barrage. The Tyrians responded with fire-ships which, despite Alexander's best precautions, immolated both structures. Undeterred he kept going, widening the great causeway and deploying more and heavier artillery. At the same time he built up his strength at sea by summoning ships from those cities which had already submitted. The Tyrians found they could not now engage at sea so used their ships to blockade their own harbours against amphibious assault.

At last the causeway reached the walls and the Macedonians' siege engines could batter the masonry. Still unbowed, the defenders threw up timber galleries and towers on top of the already formidable outer walls. They had already chucked a great raft of boulders into the coastal waters at the foot of the sheer walls to make an approach that bit harder. Alexander would have to drag these out of the way under constant harassing fire. That needed ships; the Tyrians countered by sending their own, heavily plated vessels in to cut out the attackers. Alexander up-armoured his own ships, the Tyrians then used divers to cut their cables. Alexander moved from ropes to chains, finally dragging most of the boulders clear and dumping them in deep water.

Still ready to take the offensive, the Tyrians launched a surprise naval attack on Alexander's vassals' ships blockading their north harbour. He hurried to their aid and got the better of the defenders in a sea-fight. Crowding ever closer, his ships (mounted with catapults) hammered at the walls. In the north the barrage made no real impression but in the south, cracks began to appear. Finally, a practicable breach was prised open and an attack, Gallipoli style, on improvised gangways went in. The first time round it was unsuccessful but, bit by bit, the Greeks clawed their way in through the tumbled stones and first won a bridgehead, then poured through. It was the end for the Tyrians, many of whom fought on to the last. As they had to: Alexander killed any male survivors and enslaved the rest. This was total war in its roughest guise.

Artillery could also be usefully, even decisively, deployed in the field. Arrian recounts an episode in one of Alexander's early Balkan campaigns:

> Seeing the Macedonian troops crossing the river, the natives moved down from the high ground with the intention of falling upon Alexander's party which would form the rear of the army as it withdrew; and Alexander countered by a rapid sally of his own, while the main body of his infantry, coming to the attack through the river, raised the war cry. The enemy under the combined onslaught, broke and fled, and Alexander ordered the Agrianes and archers to advance at the double to the river. He himself was the first across and, setting up his artillery on the river bank, he gave orders for every sort of missile it would take to be discharged at long range against the enemy .... (Arrian: 6)

By the time he died Alexander had led these tough hill farmers across the globe and they had followed him; men whose parents had probably never left their own settlements or journeyed much further than a few kilometres from home in their entire lives. Their marches were hard and dangerous. They faced every possible hazard – enemies, extreme cold and heat, hunger and disease. It is not surprising that finally they had enough; what is astonishing is that they went so far and endured for so long. Many became rich on booty; many others left their bones by the way or ended crippled by wounds or disease in some forgotten flea-infested outpost a very long way from anywhere. Did they see themselves as emissaries of a superior Hellenic culture? Hardly; they had simply ceased to be herdsmen and become professional soldiers – this was just what they did.

It wasn't all hard work though:

> After resting his force here he set out again and marched for seven days through the territory of Carmania, a march which son developed into a kind of Bacchanalian progression. Alexander himself feasted continually, day and night, reclining with his Companions on a dais built upon a high and conspicuous rectangular platform, the whole structure being slowly drawn along

Hoplite dekades. (By kind permission of John Conyard)

by eight horses. Innumerable wagons followed the royal table, some of them covered with purple or embroidered canopies, others shaded by the boughs of trees, which were constantly kept fresh and green; these vehicles carried the rest of Alexander's officers, all of them crowned with flowers and drinking wine. Not a single helmet, shield or spear was to be seen, but along the whole line of the march the soldiers kept dipping their cups, drinking horns or earthenware goblets into huge casks and mixing bowls and toasting one another, some drinking as they marched, others sprawled by the wayside …. (Plutarch: 67)

Macedon's later defeat and eclipse by Rome, oddly enough, was not the finish of the phalanx. In the second half of the 15th century a military revolution took place in Western Europe. The Swiss, in some ways not unlike Philip's Macedonians, had emerged from their mountain fastnesses as a force to be reckoned with. Serving as mercenaries they had come to dominate the many battlefields of the Franco-Imperialist conflict raging in northern Italy. These Swiss largely re-invented the Macedonian phalanx. Their pike columns, deployed in dense formation, stiffened by ferocious discipline and superb morale, wielded an 18-foot (5.5 metres) pike, seemed identical to the sarissa of Alexander's day.

Using mass bodies of spears was not a late medieval innovation. Robert Bruce, in 1314, a dozen years after the Flemings had routed a conventional force of mounted chivalry at Courtrai, utilised traditional Scottish formations (the *schlitron*) employing 12-foot (3.7 metres) staves to win a dazzling victory. He delivered his attacks in echelon, combining mass, momentum and cohesion in ways the Swiss would certainly have recognised. Wallace had tried the *schlitron* at Falkirk in 1298 and failed, defeated by a superior, all arms force which combined the shock of heavy cavalry with sustained missile power. In the 14th century soldiers of the emergent Swiss cantons had employed halberds to great effect winning significant victories at Mortgarten (1315) and Laupen (1339). Gradually, and partially in response to a defeat at Arbedo in 1422, the Swiss began to increase the ratio of pikes to halberds in their ranks.

This unstoppable mass of resolute points could smash through enemy formations like a steamroller, movement, mass and cohesion welded together into a formidable instrument of war. Swiss armies were characterised by relentless discipline, constant aggression and swelling confidence, by no means unlike Alexander's men. Charles the Bold of Burgundy, a daft adventurer, confronted the Swiss in the 1470s and suffered a series of catastrophic defeats, at Grandson, Morat and finally, Nancy, where his last army (and he) were slaughtered. Since then the Swiss had turned war into a trade, selling their genius for wages, which, if not forthcoming, would produce immediate defection. These Swiss fought wars as an industry, not for glory. Machiavelli was certainly impressed:

> The Swiss regiments at present are also based upon the model of the ancient phalanxes and follow their method both in closing up their order of battle and relieving their ranks; when they engage they are placed on each-other's flanks, not in a parallel line. They have no method of receiving the first rank, should it be thrown back into the second; in order to relieve each-other, they place one regiment in the front and another a little behind on the right, so if the first is hard pressed, the second may advance to its assistance, a third is placed behind both these and also on the right, at the distance of an harquebus (musket) shot. They have adopted this disposition so that if the other two are driven back, the third can advance to

relieve them, and all have sufficient room either to retreat or advance without falling foul of one another. (Machiavelli: *The Prince*)

Pike columns, as they deployed for the advance, would, from the right, comprise the van or *vorhut*. This division was followed by the main body, the *gewaltschaufen* and this, in turn supported by the rear or *nachut*. The phalanxes were fronted by harquebusiers or crossbowmen to provide covering fire together with picked swordsmen wielding hefty double-handers. Their role was to secure the vulnerable flanks of each column and act as a strike force if the main advance faltered. Momentum was the key. If this could be sustained the rush was unstoppable. But, if halted, the densely packed ranks provided a massed target. It was weight of shot that finally beat the Swiss at the decisive battle of Bicocca in 1522 – once stationary the pikemen were mown down in droves. On the borders the English achieved a comparable outcome at Pinkie in 1547. Happily, Alexander's enemies never possessed that kind of firepower!

As early as 1471, the Scots Parliament had passed an ordinance making the traditional spear redundant in favour of pikes. In 1513, their French allies were particularly keen to see the Scots adopt these winning tactics. A cadre of French officers, which disembarked at Dumbarton late in July 1513, comprised some 40 captains under the Sieur d' Aussi. Their role was to instill Swiss tactics into raw Scottish levies. This was an unenviable task, to convert such untried material into the equivalent of elite Swiss mercenaries was a formidable assignment. The time and complexity of training required to bring men up to the required standard was far more than that available to them.

For the Swiss this was their trade. They regarded war as a career. Could the companies of potentially unwilling Scottish conscripts be turned, in a matter of weeks, into a battle winning instrument? The message from Swiss victories was clear; their offensive doctrine could produce victory in the field. James IV was aware of the number of defeats Scottish spear formations had suffered in battle against the English, winnowed by bows, hacked by bills. Only an army trained and drilled in such tactics could hope to triumph.

Furthermore, to succeed the phalanx needed to be deployed on suitable ground where the momentum of attack could be sustained. Pike columns had to field men familiar with their weapon, extremely well disciplined, commanded by officers who knew their business and fired by high morale. It was common practice for commanders to attempt to use terrain to delay the rush until the enemy was at hand. A rash advance over open ground would expose the Swiss to the weight of enemy missile fire and risk fatal loss of both impetus and cohesion. Their ruthless and experienced captains appreciated the weaknesses of the puissant pike and they had developed their supporting arms accordingly. This had taken a generation, not a mere matter of weeks. The parallels with Macedon are striking; discipline is the key, small wonder the ratio of officers to men was so high.

Once Swiss brigades had been committed to battle there was little individual captains, or indeed a commander in chief, could do to further influence the outcome of the fight. Tactical flexibility was lacking and it was customary for the officers to charge home with their men. Sustaining discipline and morale were prime functions, as they were for the Macedonians. Also like them, Swiss commanders led from the front. James has been excoriated for doing just this at Flodden yet Alexander did so every time. However, the decision to lead his division in person should be viewed in the light of the prevailing doctrine. James does not appear to have attempted to throw out a skirmish line of missile troops ahead of his pike formations. These were typically used to pick off targets of opportunity and disrupt enemy lines. Charles V, a dozen years after Flodden, demonstrated their effectiveness at Pavia as the armies closed to contact.

It is generally recognised that drill, so much resented by so many generations of perhaps not too willing warriors, is a military essential. It provides the weld to cohesion and no amount of sporting or natural martial instinct can cover the deficit. This routine aspect of training is doubly essential in those who manoeuvre en masse. Here, momentum, precision and esprit largely depend upon drill instilled through months if not years of seemingly endless 'square-bashing'. It was this all-important cement that was lacking from the fabric of James' army. The men were conscripts and they had only weeks in which to train. The trouble was, he just wasn't an Alexander.

Curtius Rufus summed it up rather nicely:

> If we want a fair assessment of the Macedonians of the day, we shall have to say that the king truly deserved such subjects and his subjects such a king. (4.16.33)

CHAPTER 3

THE CORINTHIAN LEAGUE

The story goes that Alexander, upon his accession to the throne, went into the Peloponnese, where he assembled all the Greeks in that part of the country and asked them for the command of the campaign against Persia, which they had previously granted to Philip.

Arrian: 1

"'Demosthenes," he (Alexander) said, "called me a boy while I was in Illyria and among the Triballi, and a youth when I was marching through Thessaly; I will show him I am a man by the time I reach the walls of Athens"' (Plutarch: 11). He had much to prove. Philip's murder had shaken the structure of the uncertain empire he had created. He had built it; his charisma and genius had sustained it. It would be very easy for his son to lose it and for Macedon to slip back into its habitual fratricidal stew. The dust of Chaeronea had barely settled and the Greeks, while they had been subdued, were not by any means cowed. Olympias moved fast to dispose of Cleopatra Eurydice and her baby – there were no more immediate contenders. Alexander's half brother would never be a threat (it was said that he had been born perfectly healthy and his subsequent incapacity was due to poisoning by Olympias).

It was through his mother's line, she being the daughter of Neoptolemus of Epirus that Alexander had, or could certainly claim he had, the blood of Achilles flowing in his veins. He would need it. Philip had not been in any sense an emperor; more a

Fresco of an ancient Macedonian soldier in Istanbul. (DeFly94, Wikimedia Commons, CC-BY-SA-4.0)

kind of *Dux Bellorum,* a military leader. This was personal rather than inherited, so a successor would have to re-establish himself. Not, perhaps, quite from scratch but he would have to be proven. Plutarch tells us that Philip's work in Greece, bringing the city states together in a Pan-Hellenic alliance, a spear pointing towards Persia, was incomplete. He had beaten but had not yet welded the Greeks into this vital confederacy. Alexander was threatened to the south by renewed aggression led by Athens and Thebes and to the north by a resurgence of the tribes anxious to be free of the yoke Philip had imposed.

His advisors preached caution. Leave the city states to sort themselves out and buy off the wild men in the north. Alexander did the opposite. This is a theme in the classical accounts of his life. Plutarch and Arrian, echoing Ptolemy's largely lost history, are, in part at least hagiographies; Alexander is the song and they are the singers – it is all about him, the super-hero. Classical authors were not overly-troubled by modern doubts about empires and how you build them. As the action-man at the battle of the Granicus they wax lyrical about who and how many he killed in single combat, just like Achilles. The fight for the geographically elusive Persian Gates has distinct echoes of Thermopylae in reverse, except of course the Persian defenders had huge numbers, no mystical Three Hundred. Plus, of course, once outflanked, they simply ran away. The prodigy confounded them all with his bold, direct strategies.

So, he marched straightaway into Thessaly where there had been rumblings, outflanked the local forces at Tempe and was immediately elected as head of the Thessalian league. Everyone there had got the message. He blitzed a path through the symbolic narrows of the Pass at Thermopylae and the Amphictyony confirmed his place as his father's successor, as did the Congress of the Corinthian Confederacy. The smoke from his father's funeral games had barely cleared and he had already moved to assert himself. But there was more trouble brewing up north, lots of it. The Illyrians and Triballi (from what is now southern Serbia and Western Bulgaria) were restless. Their lands bordered on Macedon. He could not risk leaving this enemy unsubdued as he stripped Macedon of her fighting men and headed east. Never leave an enemy at your back.

With his now customary speed Alexander led an expedition north, pushing up unopposed until he got to a narrow pass on the lower slopes of Mount Haemus. Herodotus tells us the shrine of Dionysius was set on top of one of these and the locals intended to fight. It was a strong position and they had improvised a kind of wagon leaguer as a block. They had more wagons ready to send trundling down the pass as juggernauts to crash into the tightly packed ranks of phalangites. Alexander's remedy was for the lighter troops to simply open their order and let the vehicles thunder through harmlessly but for the denser packed ranks to lock shields and lie down, allowing the carts to just roll over them. This was a significant test of discipline and it worked. Arrian assures us '… there were no casualties'. Next he brought up his archers to shoot a barrage at the defenders as the Macedonians surged forward. This arrow storm broke up any attempt by the Thracians to attack and Alexander led his household troops in a determined assault on their left flank.

Before they came to contact the enemy decided they had had enough and bolted: 'Some 1,500 were killed but only a few captured; for most of them were too quick and knew the country too well, to fall into their enemies' hands. The women, however, who had followed the fighting men were all taken, together with the children and all the gear and stores' (Arrian: 1). This was a handy war dividend, these captives would be sold as slaves, defraying Alexander's costs. He continued his march almost to the banks of the mighty Danube.

Syrmus, king of the Triballians, had sent his non-combatants off to the refuge of Pine Tree Island in the middle of the river but the bulk of his forces tried to outflank Alexander. His scouts alerted him and he doubled back to confront them as they were making camp. The natives attempted to form up under the shelter of trees but the sting from arrows and slingshot dislodged them and Philotas led the Macedonian cavalry against their exposed right flank. He sent in his allied horsemen against their left. With both wings pinned Alexander led the phalanx straight at their centre. It was too much for the Triballians, they broke and were hunted down like rabbits as they struggled through the woods. Arrian, relying on Ptolemy, tells us 3,000 were killed for the loss of 11 cavalrymen and about 40 infantry.

Next he reached the Danube, effectively a border between the fringe of civilisation and a deep, mist-shrouded, barbarian hinterland, inhabited by the Celts. He had ships come upriver from the Black Sea Delta and he used these to have a crack at Pine Island. It proved too tough a nut so he decided to cross the river and pacify the tribes beyond. Partly this was tactics as the hostile Getae were already massing on the far bank and partly the strategy of the outward urge, this longing always to see what lay over the next range of hills, linked to his obsession with fame. Like Caesar's later crossing of the Rhine this served notice on the locals that even the vast river was no guaranteed protection.

He used those ships he had from the naval squadron, commandeered all the dugout canoes that could be found and made inflatable rafts out of his men's leather back sacks by stuffing them with hay. Arrian tells us he took 4,000 infantry and 1,500 cavalry across this way. He also crossed at night. This was no mean achievement. Once established, he marched east of the bridgehead, phalangites sweeping the summer's corn to clear a path for their mounted comrades. His logistical feat had psyched-out the Getae before a blow was struck; they did not linger much beyond the first charge. He plundered and razed their miserable town. Syrmus and many of the Celtic tribal leaders threw in their collective towels and sued for peace. These Celts were pretty impressive, fine-looking fellows. Alexander asked their envoys what they most feared in the world, thinking surely it would be him. How disappointing, it was not; instead they declared that they feared the sky might someday fall down on them. Now we know where Goscinny and Uderzo got the idea used to such good effect in the Asterix books.

As he advanced towards the territory of the Agrianes and Paeones, who lived south-east of what is now Kosovo and who had been subjugated by Philip, he learned that local warlords Cleitus and Glaucias were in open revolt. He had a respected ally in Langaros, King of the Agrianes who ably dealt with a potential threat to his line of march from the Autariates. Alexander shut Cleitus up in his stronghold of Pelium (possibly today's Gorna Gorica in Albania). Cleitus had sacrificed three boys and three girls to bring him luck, and it still wasn't working but then Glaucias arrived with a strong relief force and threatened Alexander's foragers. A show of force saw them off. Still, the defenders now outnumbered the attackers and held a ring of hills around the citadel. If Alexander tried to disengage, he risked being harried over dense, broken country.

Instead, he made a great show of force which literally frightened the enemy off the high ground. Those who remained were dislodged by a combined arms assault. Alexander disengaged in good order, got across the river and commenced his withdrawal, seeing off those of the enemy who came after. He used his artillery to keep them at a distance. Cleitus and Glaucias kept up a desultory pursuit but wrongly assumed they were chasing a beaten enemy. They were careless and Alexander struck like a cobra, launching a lightning attack on their ill-guarded camp. They were cut to pieces. Cleitus set fire to his town and made a run for it. This Balkan campaign had been a masterpiece but fresh troubles were brewing further south; potentially very serious indeed.

The Persian Emperor Darius III had been watching Alexander's Balkan campaign with interest and, doubtless, some alarm. Any hopes he and his court might have entertained that the son would prove inferior to the father, and that the threat from the west might evaporate were quickly dashed. Pursuing what we would now call hybrid warfare, a *Geltkrieg*, the Persians used their most plentiful weapon, gold. They offered Athens 300 talents to stir the pot. They should have had more sense but Demosthenes took the bung, encouraged by a rumour that Alexander and his army had been wiped out somewhere up north. Thebes, still smarting from her earlier humiliation, and irked by an army of occupation, took up arms again and besieged Alexander's garrison in the Cadmeia (the acropolis named after Cadmus, the city's alleged founder).

But Alexander was not dead, in fact he was near the town of Onchestus, only 15 miles (24 kilometres) north. They had miscalculated again and fatally. Next day he was on them. Plutarch tells us he was prepared to be reasonable, very, in the circumstances, offering to accept the surrenders of the ringleaders and let the rest off. The Thebans decided to make a fight of it anyway. They lost. Hopelessly outmatched, they were attacked from front and rear as the Macedonian garrison launched a sally. Six thousand died in the fight. Alexander took the city and wasted it, no clemency this time. The priesthood, pro-Macedonians and the family of the revered poet Pindar (just to show he had a cultured streak) got off; the rest were enslaved – 20,000 or so. The excuse for this atrocity was that he was righting wrongs done by the Thebans to other members of the Corinthian League. So the punishment was not just savagery combined with economic gain, it was a just retribution. Nobody argued.

With his enemies north and south chastised and, for the moment, completely compliant, Alexander could now embark on the great

The war council of Darius. 19th-century engraving taken from a Greek vase. By Baumeister, 1899. (Unknown, Wikimedia Commons, US Public Domain)

As per custom, the **women of Thebes** were fair game and mass-rape followed the fall. One of the victims, a woman of good family called Timocleia, was raped by a Thracian squad as they were ransacking her property. She turned the tables on their officer who she tricked into looking down the well for hidden gold then neatly tipped him down the shaft. The rest tied her and led her in front of Alexander for judgement. She was the sister of General Theagenes who had died at Chaeronea. Her looks, bearing and brave defiance won the conqueror over and she was freed, unharmed. Military historian J. F. C. Fuller uses this story as evidence Alexander was more enlightened than his contemporaries in the treatment of women. This comforting view overlooks the reality of what happened to all those other Theban women who were abused and enslaved. Alexander was utterly ruthless; this did not make him better or worse than the rest. It was the nature of the times.

project his father had instigated, the defeat and crushing of Persia. This would be the single greatest military undertaking in history. In a generation the King of Macedon had come from being an insecure opportunist to master of the classical world. What Alexander intended, as Philip had done, was to further transform their tiny upland kingdom into a world power; *the* world power.

What exactly was his plan? It is fair to suggest that Philip wished to cement his position as war leader of the Greek states, a *primus inter pares*. His strategic aim was probably to firstly liberate all those Greek cities still under Persian control and secondly to break the power of the Achaemenid dynasty for good and ever. Whether he would then have continued, firstly, to absorb that huge sprawling mass of territories and then press on and on till he ran out of space to conquer is far less certain. Philip facilitated his son's empire but the vision was Alexander's.

Who were these Persians? *Achaemenid* means one descended of Achaemenes, originally a minor 7th-century BC ruler from what is now south-western Iran and from whom Cyrus the Great claimed descent. The Achaemenids were not the original Iranian super-power; the Assyrians in the 7th century had been superseded by the Medes in the 6th. A mix of Indo-European peoples, mainly pastoral nomads, had moved into Iran around the 1st millennium BC. They had initially been dominated by the Assyrians from Mesopotamia and then the Medes. Cyrus, a man of great abilities, had thrown off Median rule and established the core of what would be the Persian Empire. He was followed by Cambyses II who extended his domination over Egypt before mysteriously vanishing among the endless sands.

A facet of Cyrus' genius was his ability to extend his rule over a widely divergent group of peoples. He respected local customs, laws and faith, but instituted strong, stable centralised government with an excellent civil service. Keeping such a diverse show on the road was never going to be easy and taxed his successors, few of whom matched his competence. The greatest symbol of empire was the opulent city of Persepolis, begun during the reign of Darius the Great but not fully completed till a century later. This was the New Delhi of the Persian Empire, a statement in stone of its wealth, power and longevity, well at least till Alexander got there.

By Alexander's day, even if the empire was getting past its sell-by date, it was still huge, Asia Minor, the Caucasus, Central Asia, territory in the Balkans, Egypt and part of what is now Libya. Alexander's ancestor, Amyntas I, had become a client in 512–511 BC as Darius the Great campaigned north of the Danube with a large army. Darius by then ruled over an empire that included Persia itself, Mesopotamia, the Levant, Cyprus, Anatolia, Armenia, the Caucasus, what is now Azerbaijan, Uzbekistan and Tajikistan, Bulgaria, Thrace, effectively Macedon, east into the Valley of the Indus and Pakistan and, of course, rich and fertile Egypt.

It was control over the Greek colonies of Asia Minor that brought Darius into conflict with the Greek city states and his efforts to chastise them turned sour in the Bay of Marathon in 490 BC. A decade later his son Xerxes came over the Hellespont to finish the job and failed. He won a pyrrhic victory at Thermopylae, burnt Athens but was defeated firstly at sea in the Bay of Salamis and then decisively on land at Plataea. Churchill might have said that while this was not the end, or even the beginning of the end, it was certainly the end of the beginning.

Artaxerxes I came to power after Xerxes' murder and abandoned direct military action for more hybrid tactics, welcoming Themistocles in exile. He used cash rather than force, building up lobbies in the fractious city states. Darius II played both sides but Cyrus the Younger funded Sparta during the latter stages of the Peloponnesian War though Egypt succeeded in temporarily wresting back her independence. Cyrus, as a younger son, resented his elder brother who became Artaxerxes II. He used his position as Satrap of Lydia to hire in 10,000 Greek mercenaries to fight for the throne. The bid failed, Cyrus was killed and Xenophon led the Greeks on their epic march. Though the Persians might not have seen it at the time this *was* the beginning of the end. 10,000 Greeks had marched across half of the Great King's domains and he had not been able to stop them. It was a dangerous precedent.

Artaxerxes reign was a golden age nonetheless. He extended and glorified Persepolis, beautified his summer capital of Ebactana, increased the influence of Zoroastrianism[1] throughout his empire, and strengthened the cult of imperial personality/divinity. The Spartans, under Agesilaus II, attacked Asia Minor so he funded Athens, Thebes and Corinth to take action against them. This sparked the Corinthian War but he then switched sides and compelled his clients to agree terms with Sparta in 386 BC. He got suzerainty of the colonies back but Sparta maintained its hegemony in Greece proper. He failed to wrest back control of Egypt but saw off a Spartan attempt to meddle in the area. He also crushed an internal revolt launched by regional satraps.

Artaxerxes died in 358 BC and was succeeded by his son of the same name, the third to rule. Insurrections flared across the empire, often funded/facilitated by the Greeks and in particular Athens. A new attempt to regain Egypt failed with Greeks providing aid and helping to fan the flames of fresh troubles. Another go at Egypt saw large numbers of Greeks fighting as mercenaries for both sides. Finally Artaxerxes triumphed and the loot from this hard won victory helped pay his bills. Having won back the Nile he then suppressed the various internecine squabbles still smoldering within his vast territories. For the moment that seemed to be it. His general Bagoas who had done good service enjoyed a rapid rise.

Philip's even more meteoric rise attracted Artaxerxes' attention and he viewed the ascendancy of this new, if unlikely, Pan-Hellenic champion with growing alarm. He sent support to Philip's enemies in Thrace and it was perhaps this which gave rise to or crystallised the grand concept of a Greek invasion of Persia. Artaxerxes did not live to see this, his murderously ambitious subordinate Bagoas poisoned him in 338 BC. His successor, the fourth Artaxerxes, went the same way practically before he had his backside on the imperial throne as did anyone else who might have had any kind of claim, almost a massacre. Bagoas placed a fellow governor, Darius, onto the hot seat thinking he could control him but the protégé promptly forced yet more poison down his sponsor's neck and took

---

1 Zarathustra, an Iranian prophet and religious reformer flourished before the 6th century BC (he is more widely known outside Iran by his Greek name, Zoroaster). Zoroastrianism contains both monotheistic and dualistic features. It likely influenced the other major Western religions including Judaism, Christianity and Islam.

the throne as Darius III. If Darius had had access to a crystal ball, he might have thought twice.

Now Macedon was poised to lead Greece in a final showdown with Persia.

It is logistics that matter most in war, especially in expeditionary warfare. Alexander, even when campaigning as far as the Danube was to an extent fighting on interior lines. Asia was completely different; it would be the enemy who had that advantage. Depending on which account you believe, he would lead between 30,000–43,000 infantry and 4,000 cavalry over the Hellespont. If we think that a Great War infantry battalion of 1,000 men required a mile of road, that's a tail of over 40 miles for the infantry alone, more space for the cavalry, then all of the tents, provisions and baggage, the sappers with all their tools and kit plus an artillery train. In all probability when you add on the camp followers, ancillary trades etc, the Macedonian army stretched for 100 miles.

The phalangite would have empathised with Marius' Mules (of the late Roman Republic). Alexander's men were now paid professionals and did not need pampering. They carried their own kit – virtually all of it, armour, helmet, weapons, tools, personal gear and rations. This immensely sped up the line of marching, though the men surely groaned and groused beneath their mighty loads. It is a shame Alexander's classical biographers were more into derring-do than nuts and bolts logistics because that's ultimately what wins wars.

Publius Flavius Vegetius Renatus wrote his classic *Epitome of Military Science* sometime in the late 4th or early 5th century, many centuries after Alexander. Yet much of what he says would have applied to the Greek Army. Vegetius was in no doubt that such tough love paid dividends:

> In every battle it is not numbers and untaught bravery so much as skill and training that generally produce the victory. For we see no other explanation of the conquest of the world by the Roman People than their drill-at-arms, camp-discipline and military expertise. How else could small Roman forces have availed against hordes of Gauls? How could small stature have ventured to confront German tallness? (Vegetius: 1.1)

This was a new type of soldier then, as much the armed extension of the body corporate as an individual warrior. His loyalty was primarily to the state but all too often this transferred to the person of his commanding general who would lead him, hopefully, to victory and to riches. Alexander combined both, he *was* the state. The fortunes of each individual soldier depended on his commander's success. This forged a strong personal bond but the phalangite was still a tough, independent minded, and, not infrequently cantankerous, individual, ready and vociferous with their grousing. The general might be in charge but he was no Olympian. Alexander had the great commander's gift of getting his men to love him, though he finally wore them out.

Relentless training implied the men would be able to adopt whichever fighting order best suited the ground and the nature of the threat as it emerged. Good soldiers are not automata, they respond through training and instinct. We talk about 'a soldier's battle' and many of Alexander's fights were just that. In close country in the whirling melee of ambush or sudden contact, the general cannot actually control the melee; he has to rely on the capacities of his men.

This is the essence of war, something which Alexander understood. Successful command is not all about tactics. In some ways these may be regarded as a given. Victory is brought about through logistics and the ability to concentrate; through what Rupert Smith calls, 'the utility of force'. The general who can ensure he has his forces in the right place at the right time: ensure they are fed, watered, supplied, supported and motivated, has already come a long way towards success. The infantryman instinctively understands this. He knows all about hard marching and the hollowness of an empty belly. He won't tolerate fools and is not shy about voicing an opinion. Officers are to be obeyed, even feared and sometimes revered but they never God-like or unchallengeable.

When it came to manoeuvring for battle, open ground was always to be preferred, bare of cover or impediment, ideally sloping to add momentum to the charge when it came: 'This is judged the more advantageous, the higher the ground occupied. For weapons descend with more violence onto men on a lower level, and the side which is higher dislodges those opposing them in greater force. He who struggles uphill enters a double contest with the ground and with the enemy' (Vegetius, III. 13). This changes if the infantry are facing cavalry where more broken ground which can disorder the enemy charge is preferred, naturally for your own cavalry, you would favour a clear run.

Trees were not liked. The astonishingly incompetent Quinctilius Varus danced to the tune of his nimble foe Arminius in the forests of Germany in AD 9 and led his Roman legions to annihilation at the hands of enemies who, on open ground, they would have trounced in an hour. Command and control, essential tools for victory, could not be properly exercised out of sight. Controlling a classical era battle once the troops were committed was no easy matter at the best of times. The commanding general needed to see how his units were performing and be able to adapt his plan to circumstances. Once that function became obscured it was lost.

For the Macedonian infantryman, pioneering was a daily task. Every night he dug a fortified encampment, surrounded by ditch and palisade, the heavy leather tents, one for each section, laid out in precisely the same order. The camp resembled a permanent fort, gates facing north, south, east and west. The commander's tent was always pitched centrally with his officers ranged on both sides; infantry, cavalry and allies/auxiliaries knew their places. Uniformity made for efficiency, cohesion and constant readiness.

At reveille, tents were struck, then loaded onto baggage animals and finally, as the army was about to move off, the camp was leveled. The men shouted out in response to the herald's call that they were ready to march. Three times the call to arms was repeated and the column stepped forward. Pioneers marched near the front to clear obstacles and ensure smooth passage for the army. The officer's baggage, precious as ever, came behind, followed by the commander in chief with his personal escort. Next rode the rest of the cavalry, followed by the mule train.

After them the rest of the senior officers with their bodyguards and then the bulk of infantry forces, each led by the standards, all marching four-abreast. Allied units, if any were serving, formed the rear with a tail of cavalry and probably some infantry. Above all the

The Greek/Macedonian military **diet** was very similar to civilian fare; cereals such as barley, emmer wheat and einkorn augmented by lentils, peas and chickpeas. These were cheap and plentiful to procure and could be dry-stored for long periods. The cereals were used in making gruel (kykeon), bread, groats and flat cakes. Soups and stews were mostly vegetable, meat would have been something of a luxury. Officers undoubtedly enjoyed rather more and varied rations. Xenophon tells us: 'The following day Koiratadas appeared with animals for offerings and a seer, carrying barley flour with them, twenty with wine, three with a load of olives, one with a large amount of garlic, as much as he was able to carry, and finally one with a huge amount of onions' (Xenophon: vii.I.37). They drank water and wine. Poorer men had a cheaper brew made from water and grape residue mixed with lees. The army could buy or requisition supplies as it moved but keeping such a large host fed was a Sisyphean task at all times.

army feared being attacked when deployed in column and the order of march would be varied to reflect the nature and likely direction of the perceived threat. All of them had to be fed. Most importantly the horses needed constant fodder and access to fresh water. Foraging parties were out constantly, supply dumps in friendly territory amassed. The commissariat was the most important department.

So Alexander of Macedon stands on the shore of Asia, in front of him is a vast empire stretching to infinity. His father was a man who became a hero and heroes can become gods. Alexander was already a hero ...

CHAPTER 4

OVER THE HELLESPONT

And Caesar's spirit, ranging for revenge,
With Ate by his side come hot from hell,
Shall in these confines with a monarch's voice
Cry 'Havoc!' and let slip the dogs of war

Shakespeare: *Julius Caesar* Act 3: I

Alexander had not just shown himself to be his father's worthy heir and successor; he had proven himself as a general and as a king – and he was still only twenty. But what he was now to attempt was in an altogether different league. In his favour: not all the Asian side was hostile. To the Greek city states which Persia had controlled for so long, this was deliverance. For Alexander, they would offer secure bases would ease his supply chain, his army would be passing through potentially friendly territory. He faced two main threats. The first was a large enemy force, certainly equal in size, if less certain in qualitive terms, massing under local, provincial governors on the banks of the Granicus River. The second was the potential maritime threat from naval forces operating on the Levant coast.

His own fleet was about 200 strong. Used to ferry his army over the Hellespont, many of these vessels were transports rather than men o'war and the Phoenicians would likely have rather more. He could not afford to leave this threat to the homeland unchecked. His strategic aim was to neutralise the risk by taking out the enemy's shore bases, the great harbours of Lebanon.

Occupy the ports, control the shipyards and the dragon's teeth would be pulled.

Plutarch tells us Alexander had doled out royal sinecures and renders to his companions, not just buying their ongoing support but showing he was determined to win fresh kingdoms in the east and that his manifest destiny lay there. Before he proceeded he had to visit Troy and do due homage at his hero's tomb, perform the necessary rites and run races around the barrow. There was policy in this too. Achilles had humbled the Trojans, the parallel was obvious. Now Alexander was here to do the same, indeed to surpass his hero's achievements. The Achilles brand was an important brick in the building of Alexander's own. Clearly he did identify with the hammer of Troy but this was only the start of his own legend. He couldn't just be Philip's son, he needed to build up a cult of personality around himself and the myth of Achilles, already totemic, was the best starting point.

Strategically, he had to secure his open seaward flank while eliminating the threat to the east posed by these large opposition forces. Until he had dealt with these, his southerly advance could not continue. He threw out a screen of scouts and skirmishers to be his eyes and ears and undoubtedly organised spies in their camp. The Persian army wasn't all Persian, not by any means; a big part of their infantry force was made up of Greek hoplite mercenaries (said to be 20,000 of them, though this is very likely a significant exaggeration[1]) under the formidable Memnon of Rhodes and they had lots of cavalry. Their position lining the far bank of the swift flowing river was a good one, ideal for defence. Any attacker would have to ford the river which, while doable, would be no easy matter

---

1 Numbers overall are hard to define with any accuracy. Alexander would have had approximately 1,700 Macedonian Companion (elite) cavalry and over 3,000 from the allies, a mix of heavy and light troops. The phalanx probably numbered around 12,000, plus 7,000 allied hoplites, 3,000 Macedonian heavy infantry (hypaspists), with another 12,000 allied light infantry (*peltasts*) and a thousand or so missile troops drawn from Agriana (javelins) and Crete (archers). The Persians could likely field over 15,000 in various mounted contingents, about 8,000–10,000 mercenary hoplites and several thousand Persian infantry of varying types, (from Wharry, J., *Warfare in the Classical World* (London; Salamander 1980), p. 70).

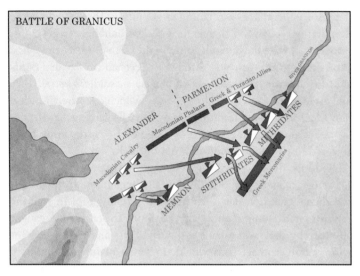

The battle of the Granicus River, 334 BC. (Chloe Rodham)

especially under a deluge of missiles and then scramble up a steep, wet bank to come to grips.

Parmenion, who had been in Asia Minor longer in joint command of the vanguard counseled caution. Attalus had been the other joint commander until his execution on Alexander's orders: a fate that, in time, also awaited Parmenion. The water was too deep, the river banks too high, it was too late in the day and besides it was the wrong time of year.[2] But Alexander did not do caution; he was determined to attack. Strategically this made sense: strike a significant blow at the enemy this early on and Asia Minor would open up like a tin of sardines.

Tactically, it was going to be challenging. Alexander stuck to his standard formula; the infantry would pin the Persian centre while massed cavalry on the Macedonian right wing would deliver the decisive blow (see map above). Parmenion would lead the left wing and his son Philotas would be brigade commander on the right,

---

2 It was May/June, the Macedonian month of Daesius. Traditionally the Macedonians did not fight then, probably because it was harvest time, but this was a new type of warfare.

the cavalry flank. This was bound to get messy. There would be no thundering Hollywood charge; the Greeks would have to get across the wet gap, scale the difficult banks in the teeth of the enemy's best efforts then grind their way through the Persian cavalry in a battle of attrition – the mounted version of a classic soldier's battle. They had more body armour and longer lances which conferred an edge. Plus Alexander would lead them in person, the galvanising effect of his heroic presence so often the tipping point. On the other hand he could just get killed and that would be that.

Diodorus disagrees with Plutarch and Arrian here. He says Alexander made his approach at night, reconnoitered the fords and then attacked at dawn which could certainly explain why the Persian's Greek hoplites were lagging behind. The enemy was caught off guard by the dawn assault and most of the phalangites had got across before contact (this would, in terms of inherent military probability, make good tactical sense). Plutarch is adamant the battle began late afternoon. We suspect Diodorus was right though.

Alexander would be the most obvious target; that year's must-kill celebrity. No Alexander, no conquest and Persia would be safe for a generation at least. When Cyrus previously went down at Cunaxa that ended his war. And, of course, Alexander would be dressed up to the nines, not hard to spot. Scouts would have eyed up the river, sussed out the most fordable places. It was something of a race, Persian cavalry and light troops were lining the far bank while their heavy, Greek infantry lagged some way behind. While the wet gap was not any real obstacle for the Macedonian vanguard, comprised of agile light horsemen beefed up with a squadron of 'heavies' drawn from the elite Companions, there could be no charge. The steep slither up the wet sides was met with a regular storm of arrows and javelins. Casualties were heavy.

Alexander's whole line was deployed obliquely, cavalry leading on the right, then the heavy Macedonian infantry forming a hinge with the phalanx slanting towards the left. That flank was held by the allied hoplites and Thessalian cavalry:

> There was a profound hush as both armies stood for a while motionless on the brink of the river, as if in awe of what was to come. Then Alexander, while the Persians still waited for the

crossing to begin, that they might fall upon his men as they were struggling up the further bank, leapt upon his horse and called upon his bodyguard to follow and to play the man. His orders were that Amyntas, son of Arrabeus, should lead off into the water with the advanced scouts, the Paeonians, and one infantry company, preceded by Ptolemy[3] son of Philip, with Socrates' squadron, which was the leading cavalry squadron for that day; then he himself, at the head of the right wing of the army, with trumpets blaring and the shout going up to the God of battle, moved forward into the river. (Arrian: I.15)

For a while it hung in the balance. Alexander's men had a tough challenge to get up that treacherous bank and engage. Once his forces were committed there was not much a classical era commander could do to affect the outcome. King James IV of Scotland has been showered with opprobrium for doing at Flodden exactly what Alexander did at the Granicus, leading like a company officer rather than a commanding general and monarch. It got James and a very large number of his subjects killed. It could easily have done the same for Alexander but his luck held.

Every Persian warrior really, really, wanted to be the man who killed Alexander of Macedon. The tall nodding plumes of his gorgeous helmet marked him out, a javelin glanced off his breastplate, penetrating the bronze but not his flesh. Plutarch also tells us two of Darius' local commanders, Rhoesacses and Spithridates, took him on. He dodged the latter's lunge and used his lance against the first but the point sheared off against the man's armour and snapped, so Alexander drew his sword. Spithridates took a swing at his head, hacked off one of the plumes and cracked the helmet, grazing the king's skull.

As he got ready for another go, 'Black' Cleitus, commander of Alexander's household troop, impaled the Persian at the same time as the king accounted for Rhoesacses with his kopis. Arrian names the same two opponents but reverses who kills who. Either way,

---

3 Ptolemy I 'Soter' (Saviour) was a childhood friend and trusted subordinate, one of Alexander's successors and founder of the Ptolemaic dynasty in Egypt. He may have been a half brother – one of Philip's illegitimate children.

they still end up dead. This is all very Homeric and may, in fact, have originally come from the pen of Alexander's court historian Callisthenes, copied by the classical writers pretty much verbatim. Such Hollywood feats would read very well at the time and we can be sure Achilles would have thoroughly approved.

Winning a toehold, a bridgehead, was vital. As the forlorn hope struggled up the slope, the rest of the companions followed led by the king himself, Achilles proper in action. At the same time the allied cavalry, Thessalians under Calas, allied squadrons led by Philip and Thracians commanded by Agathon, repeated the process on the Greek left. A desperate series of very untidy melees followed. On the right as Alexander bulldozed a path, the hypaspists marched on as did the brigades of phalangites, led by Craterus, Meleager and Philip.

The Persian infantry were no match and soon both flanks gave way, routing back towards the Greek mercenaries who held their ground, prior to attempting a withdrawal. More than half were trapped and surrounded on a low hillock. They offered to yield but Alexander was not interested. This lot were not just the enemy, they were traitors and needed to be made an example of. They were, only 2,000 survived and they were all captured. No prisoner of war status here, they were sent back in chains to Macedon for use as slave labour in the mines, their sweat and blood helping to fund the ongoing campaign. The fight was over: Macedonians 1, Persians 0.

Plutarch puts the Persians' losses at over 20,000, a suspiciously high figure against 34 Macedonians, only nine of whom were infantry. Arrian states 25 elite Macedonian cavalry were lost, with 60 more from the allies and 30 footsoldiers. The disproportion is pretty striking. We know Alexander commissioned Lysippus to cast bronze memorials for each of the dead companions. One could hazard a guess that the classical chroniclers were offering a propagandist tally of Greek casualties – you could reasonably reduce the Persian losses by a very high percentage. Alexander sent 300 sets of Persian harness, taken from the dead, to Athens as a token of his victory and as a timely reminder of what happened to those who defied him: 'Alexander, son of Philip, and the Greeks (except the

Sparta was sidelined or rather had sidelined itself; the city state had not fought against Philip and not bemoaned the sack of Thebes. It was Epaminondas who had destroyed Sparta's hegemony. Having kept out of the Corinthian League, Sparta was still ready to take Darius' subsidies and launch a second front in Greece while Alexander was away. It had a go at Crete between 333–332 BC and failed. Their king, Agis, decided to try and stir the Peloponnese the year after. Athens would have none of it, nor would the Arcadians; giving Antipater the balcony he needed to launch a pre-emptive blow, raising the Spartan siege of Megalopolis (now Megalopoli in south-west Arcadia) which had also refused to join the conspiracy. He killed Agis in the process, striking the head from the snake. That was the last heard from Sparta for a while.

Lacedaemonians [Spartans]) dedicate these spoils, taken from the Persians who dwell in Asia' (Arrian: 17). This was stick and carrot; he would happily share the spoils with his fellow Greeks just as long as they remembered who was head of the table.

The battle of the Granicus was a remarkable and relatively bloodless victory; now Greek mercenaries would think twice before signing up for Darius. Among the Persian dead lay their leaders Niphates, Petines and, of course Spithridates; one of Darius' sons, a son-in-law and brother-in-law. More recent commentators have suggested that the whole Homeric passage of single combats has significant echoes of *The Iliad* while the more general tactics are ignored. *The Iliad* has Achilles leap into the River Scamander hunting more Trojans to kill: Alexander's court historian Callisthenes (on whom the classical authors subsequently relied) cynically offered the comparison in writing up the single combat episode.

This stunning victory produced what we would now call a domino effect. Most of the great cities of the region were ethnically Greek and hungering for freedom from Persian domination. Sardis, capital of ancient Lydia, said to have been founded by the sons of Hercules, opened its gates, throwing them wide without a fight. Eight miles from the walls the local Persian commander rode out to discuss terms. Alexander treated everyone well. Other key settlements followed till Halicarnassus (now modern Bodrum) and Miletus were the only ones holding out. Part of the *casus belli* for the whole campaign was to liberate the Greek city states in Asia Minor. Allowing them to maintain their democratic customs was important, showing they were not just getting a new tyrant in place of the old. The Persian garrison at Ephesus took to their ships and bolted. However Halicarnassus, occupying a key site on the Ceramic coast, was a major naval base which did not fall till autumn 334 BC. Losing such a strategically important centre further dented Darius' capacity to mount maritime operations against Greece and Macedon.

Defending Halicarnassus was Memnon of Rhodes, the Greek mercenary officer who had commanded the hoplites at the Granicus. He had offered more Fabian tactics, avoiding battle, but the satraps had overruled him and now most were dead. He had not lost credibility; in fact his stock had gone up. He had endeavoured to hold Miletus but Alexander moved too fast, getting his ships into the harbour before the Persian fleet could dock. They still enjoyed a significant numerical advantage in a sea fight and for once it was Alexander who demurred when Parmenion suggested taking them on. Some of the citizens of the town suggested an armistice whereby Miletus became a kind of open city with joint jurisdiction. It was a nice try but Alexander's response was an assault the next day when he took the place.

Memnon and his hired guns got away and fell back on Halicarnassus. He intended to make a fight of it, losing the place would be a disaster and it was a very strong position. Alexander was ready for a lengthy siege. He filled in the defensive ditch to bring his siege towers close to the walls and saw off a night sortie. A pair of Macedonian soldiers, full of drink, mounted their own private attack and, with others backing them almost forced an entry but the breaches were sealed off and the fight went on. It was a slow process of attrition, the walls were steadily weakened, the garrison's fighting capacity eroded. Memnon and his fellow officers finally decided it was time to get out and withdrew their survivors at night with incendiaries spreading fire through the doomed town as a distraction.

Once he became aware of what was going on Alexander immediately ordered a general assault, despite the fact it was still dark. He took the place, or whatever was left of it. Memnon had occupied some strong outposts which he could not hope to hold so made his escape by sea. Alexander flattened what was left of Halicarnassus as a message to anyone else thinking of resistance and moved on, leaving a female governor in charge – again, this was in harmony with local custom.

Memnon was not done though. He attempted to establish forward operating bases on some of the Aegean islands. This might be dangerous, a spear aimed at Macedon and perhaps a rally point for those Greeks not too enamoured of Macedonian rule. He took Chios, most of Lesbos and besieged the island's main city, Mitylene. Happily for Macedon, he died suddenly and those who succeeded him lacked the same drive. They did take Mitylene but when Antipater sent out a naval squadron to shoo them away, they went.

Meanwhile Alexander continued on what appeared a triumphal progress. He had neutralised the threat to both flanks and Parmenion had the bulk of the army in safe quarters in mighty Sardis, a cushy billet. As he advanced Alexander took the city of Xanthus in Lycia where providentially an ancient inscribed tablet surfaced from a nearby spring, foretelling the doom of Persia at the hands of Greeks. Next he kept pushing south towards Cilicia (that region of Turkey lying north-east of Cyprus) and Phoenicia.

His march was not interrupted. He outdid Canute: the waves receded obligingly to allow his easy passage along the coastal fringe. Still unopposed, Alexander continued with just a striking force around the southern coast of Asia Minor to rendevous with the main body at Gordium. Here he was able to take on reinforcements sent from Macedon. Arrian tells us these included another 3,000 heavy infantry, 300 horsemen, rather fewer allied cavalry and some additional allied light infantry. These would help make good losses from battle and those left on garrison duty.

On a more strategic note, he marched his combined forces northward to cow the peoples of Cappadocia (central Anatolia) and Paphlagonia (on the Black Sea coast of north central Anatolia). Memnon was, by now, dead and the threat he posed to the home

Capital of ancient Phrygia, Gordium was the city of fabled King Midas (located around 70–80 kilometres south-west of present day Ankara). Here Alexander found a knotty problem. An ancient chariot was lashed onto its yoke by a very complex knot tied from the bark of the cornel-tree. Legend asserted that whoever could untie the mystical knot would end up as ruler of the world (meaning, in that context, the Persian Empire). Well, obviously Alexander just had to have a go. He solved the problem in his usual direct way, either by just slashing the fibres with his sword or, more subtly, pulling out the yoke pin so that shaft slid free and the ends of the ties were exposed and so easily undone. Cutting the **Gordian knot** may seem just like a dash of propaganda to us but it mattered in a deeply superstitious age when portents and prophecies had deep significance. Such gestures were almost as important in undermining Darius' authority as victories in the field.

front largely died with him. Though Alexander refused, at least for the moment, to free those Athenian mercenaries he had captured earlier. Meanwhile, Darius had not been entirely idle. He had conscripted a vast army from the rump of his empire, said by Plutarch to have been 600,000 strong.

We can probably move the decimal point on this one but it was still an awfully large force. He had had a helpful dream assuring him of victory which tells you something about wishful thinking. But he had to act. With the western flank now secure and most of Asia Minor under his thumb, it was only a matter of time before Alexander came looking for him in the deep interior. Darius could not afford to simply wait. His own prestige had been badly dented by the earlier defeat and he now had no hope of opening a second front against Macedon from home waters.

Alexander's seeming inactivity was not due to faintheartedness. He had been ill, dangerously so. At this time far more soldiers died of disease than from wounds. Typhus and dysentery stalked armies with the assurance of a grim reaper. Plutarch suggests Alexander might also have been brought low through exhaustion. That sounds feasible. Both Plutarch and Arrian mention Alexander's plunge into the cold River Cydnus for a swim and the chill he contracted as a result. His illness was dangerous; his death would mean the end of the campaign, of the war. Some of his physicians were afraid to administer drugs in case their patient did succumb and they were blamed. One who did dare was Philip the Arcanian. Alexander had received intelligence that his doctor planned to poison him and read this out to Philip as he drank the potion, as an indication of his trust – which was not misplaced, he made a full recovery.

Darius made his move. Despite a warning from a Macedonian traitor, Amyntas, who knew only too well how formidable Alexander was, he moved his great sprawling host forwards. He came down from the north, through a mountain pass known as the Amanian Gates (now in south-western Turkey) to the city of Issus (an ancient coastal settlement straddling the River Pinarus and in the lee of difficult uplands). He was now behind Alexander who had used the place as a base hospital and depot. Darius casually killed any wounded left behind. Tactically, the move was foolish: the hemmed in ground would prevent the Persian from deploying his superior numbers to better effect. Amyntas had advised him to wait, to let the Greeks advance and then fight them on the broad central plains where there was ample ground for manoeuvre. But Darius had set the stage; it remained to see how well he could dance.

Alexander had sent a galley back up the coast to check out Darius' dispositions and these naval scouts were able to confirm not only his presence but the enormous size of his army. The Great King was set to make a fight of it and this would be a big one. It was also just what Alexander wanted – a decisive battle. Arrian tells us Alexander promptly summoned all his officers to a briefing and rounded off with a good Agincourt style address: 'Remember … that already danger has threatened you and you have looked it triumphantly in the face; this time the struggle will be between a victorious army and an enemy already once vanquished. God himself, moreover, by suggesting to Darius to leave the open ground and cram his great army into a confined space, has taken charge of operations on our behalf' (Arrian: 2.7). He goes on, rightly to remind them, that the confined ground will work to the Macedonians advantage and Darius' numbers will be just a hindrance. He tells them the Medes and Persians have grown soft from too much easy living while the Greeks are hardy, 'lean and hungry men'. Above all the Macedonians are free citizens and not slaves. This was ironic as Alexander was as absolute a ruler but great military oratory does not get tangled up in inconvenient detail. He pointed out their allies were also top notch but above all, the Macedonians had Alexander!

CHAPTER 5

KING IN SPLENDOUR

There are only a few people in history who are universally known as 'the Great', and Alexander of Macedon, who reigned and conquered much of the known world between 336 and 323 B.C., probably tops the list. The word 'great' in this context, to my mind, is always positive – implying both that Alexander's achievements were huge in scale, and that his nature was heroic and awe-inspiring.

James Romm, *Two Great Historians on Alexander the Great*, Part 1
(Forbes online, retrieved 8 May 2018)

Arrian gushes over Alexander's rousing oratory. Much of this is probably fiction; an army of over 20,000 is not likely to hear a single voice, even if the speech was delivered the day before battle. Besides, the time for talking was long past. Still, Arrian tells us that Alexander reminded them of the great fruits and spoils of victory (always goes down a treat), and he also reminded them of Xenophon's achievement, that the whole of Asia was theirs when they won. Modesty notwithstanding, he extoled his own glorious conquests. He might have been slighter than Darius and not perhaps as good looking but he was a winner not a loser. Having seen to his men's rations, he marched them through the narrow pass linking to the coastal plain and deployed, shaking his brigades out into line, as soon as the ground allowed.

'Alea iacta est' (the die is cast) as Julius Caesar would say much later. And it was. Darius had chosen a position not dissimilar to that taken by his satraps at the Granicus though he had, to a degree, stolen a march on Alexander by cutting off his line of retreat. But the King of Macedon was not retreating and Darius had in fact played to Alexander's game plan by committing his huge host to battle, doing so on ground which inhibited free deployment of his vastly superior numbers. The wet gap lay between him and the Macedonian army; he did not intend to attack. They must come at him.

Alexander was happy to oblige. The topography of the coastal plain enabled Darius to refuse both flanks; low hills rising on his left and the sea to his right. The plain was two miles (3.2 kilometres) across. The River Pinarus ran laterally along the Persian front line and he had thrown a cloud of skirmishers forward as a screen, masking his dispositions. Cavalry was deployed on both flanks, with a strongly posted line of heavy infantry in the centre. From left to right this comprised of 10,000 Persian troops armed like Greek hoplites (*cardaces*), with 8,000–10,000 Greek mercenaries in the middle, then a similarly sized division of *cardaces* standing left of them. Behind this front line milled a great huge mass of Persian levies – perhaps as many as 50,000, arrayed in their national or regional units. Arrian claims the forces Darius had sent across the river as his defensive screen amounted to 20,000 infantry and 30,000 cavalry which seems a suspiciously high total, particularly for the *arme blanche* but we may assume their overall numbers were still very substantial. This Persian array must have been impressive, braying trumpets and proud, brilliant banners fluttering, a seemingly unstoppable horde of biblical proportions, like the population of a dozen major cities on the move. This gorgeous fighting array would have trailed an even bigger crowd of followers, drawn from every nation under Darius' domination. It was an astonishing spectacle and nobody on the Greek side had ever seen anything remotely like it.

Once more, Alexander relied on his standard deployment. He massed the phalanx; 12,000 phalangites on his left centre, each brigade led by a trusted subordinate with Parmenion as divisional commander. The bulk of the cavalry were concentrated for the big blow on their right; 2,100 Companions, roughly the same number

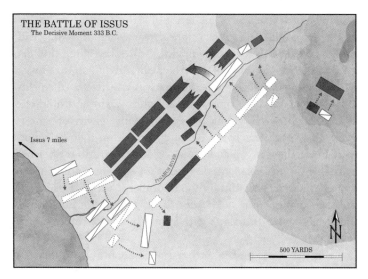

The battle of Issus, 333 BC. (Chloe Rodham)

of Thessalians, then perhaps 1,600 mounted allies. The hinge on the cavalry's left was formed by the elite *hyspaspists,* 3,000 strong, under Parmenion's son, Nicanor, with another 7,000 allied heavies and about 12,000 assorted light infantry and skirmishers.

Before contact Darius decided the rising ground on his right was unfavourable and, in tactical terms, a waste of so many horsemen, so shifted the bulk of his cavalry onto his left. At the same time, he recalled the mounted troops earlier sent over the river. Alexander conformed in turn by switching more allied cavalry to his left and extended his remaining Companion squadrons to close the gap, supported by a screen of skirmishers able to move easily on the uneven, rising ground. He ordered the cavalry to move discreetly behind the massed sarissas so the enemy could not detect the shift. Alexander was by now aware of the threat to his right where he was in danger of being outflanked, so echeloned a couple of the Companion's units with supporting light infantry to conform. The stage was now set.

None, or certainly few (some survivors from the earlier fight were in the ranks) of these Persians had seen the Macedonians deploy before. That incredible forest of sarissas must have looked utterly daunting, a great, steel tipped steamroller, brimming with confidence, drilled, professional and ready. Like rolling thunder, the phalanx moved forward over the plain, driving on the Persian skirmishers, whose deluge of missiles was met by raised shields. This would take some time – the distance was over a mile (1.5 kilometres) between, giving the Persian centre plenty of time to move up to the river bank. Keeping formation, the phalangites waded over the wet gap and came to contact, a furious desperate fight. Darius had planted the cream of his great army in the centre, where they significantly outnumbered their attackers. He had the sloping nature of the river bank to work for him and he had strengthened this slope with timber palisades thrown up at key points.

This is the classic push of sarissa against hoplite armed infantry, Greek mercenaries and Persians, a howling stamping melee, noise crashing like breakers on the shore, great clouds of steam and dust rising as the lines collide, shift, buckle and brace. The men on the right had seen off the threat for the moment and consolidated their position, Alexander brought some of them back to his other flank to bolster his strike force. Parmenion's advance had created a gap between the Macedonian brigades, one the enemy could exploit while the remaining Persian cavalry crashed into the Thessalians and their supporting light infantry. The line wavered but held. This infantry duel was fierce. Darius' Greek mercenaries were only too well aware of their fate if they ran or tried to surrender. They, more so even than the Immortals, were the pick of his vast motley army and the determined phalangites, strain as they might, could not budge them.

For a time, this was the crucible of the fight, a thrusting, groaning, hacking brawl. Firstly, there was the noise – battles even before firearms were not quiet. The great stamping mass of men generated vast sound and furnace heat, the temperature in the melee a dozen degrees higher. Men poured out sweat in rivulets, steam likes a blast furnace and there are huge, great cloying clouds of dust. It was disorientating; a man in the ranks would have no idea what was going on more than a metre away. Helmets, whilst

The shock troops of the Persian Empire were the **'Immortals'**, a division of heavy infantry whose strength was always kept at exactly 10,000 men. They may have got their name from the fact that if a man died in action or retired, he was immediately replaced so the corps strength never declined. They, like the later Ottoman janissaries, had specific and near universal kit. They wore headdresses and scale armour over arming jackets with a range of personal weapons, bows, stabbing or throwing spears, short thrusting swords, waisted shields, slings and even axes. On the march they had their own rear echelon of baggage carts and wagons to carry gear, loot and a supply of women. They provided the strike force for Cambyses II's conquest of Egypt in 525 BC, then served Darius I in a series of campaigns along the north-west frontier of India and as far east as mysterious Scythia. Their name was recycled in the following centuries. As late as the 1970s the last Shah of Iran kept an all arms brigade dubbed the Immortals, 5,000–7,000 strong with an integral tank battalion. They continued to serve until the revolution of 1979, after which they were disbanded.

essential, impeded sight and hearing. And then there were the smells, none too fragrant. Wounds came sudden and terrible, death was generally caused by blows to the head but strikes against the torso could cause deep sucking chest wounds or evisceration and limbs could be mangled or sheared. These men knew how to kill. Anyone who went down before the rush of sarissas, if he showed any sign of vitality, would be dispatched by a backwards jab of the butt of the sarissa, neatly drilling the skull, though it would not have looked all that neat.

Next, at the head of his riders, Alexander threw his own left-wing cavalry against the beefed-up Persian right and a horseman's battle erupted. This was just as untidy as the infantry fight. Once both sides came to contact, it swiftly degenerated into a swirl of personal and small unit scrapping. The Macedonians with heavier kit and longer lances again had an advantage but Alexander took a tremendous risk by leading in person. It was difficult, if not downright impossible, for the classical era field commander to direct events once battle was joined, especially if he committed himself to lead in person. Alexander was a gambler; all successful generals are. There is a theory that successful leaders have an innate sixth sense in judging timing and odds and a degree of nerve to carry it through. If so, Alexander had this in spades and, unlike Darius, he had the inestimable, even crucial, advantage of being able to rely on seasoned and skilled subordinates, old hands like Parmenion who knew their work and how to see it through.

Alexander's personal leadership and the superior quality of his troopers proved decisive: the Persian cavalry on that flank were driven off. This defection left that wing of the *cardaces* exposed. Moreover, Darius with his staff and household, stationed behind the main line, became increasingly vulnerable. Alexander naturally went after the king, whom the Immortals rushed in to defend. Taking the king was checkmate. But these were crack troops and they held their ground. Alexander himself was wounded in the thigh during the melee. Some accounts assert he got the cut from Darius personally with whom he was sparring but Plutarch is dubious. He points out that Alexander, when subsequently reporting in correspondence with Antipater, makes no mention of a personal encounter, not something he would be likely to omit. Nonetheless, Darius is the one who suffered a crisis of leadership and took the chance to make a run for it, his royal chariot galloping off the field as fast as possible.

Like a line of dominos, the whole Persian line began to unravel. Cheated of Darius, the cavalry smashed into the heavy infantry on the Persian left who gave way, allowing the hard-pressed Macedonian phalanx to surge forward. Alexander's Companions now turned their lances against those Greek mercenaries still doggedly contesting the centre. Pretty soon they were completely isolated as the remaining *cardaces* bolted, taking the second line with them. Hemmed in both by cavalry and the left-hand division of the phalanx, the Greeks were forced to give ground and try to bend their line to meet these new threats. This meant they lost the advantage of the slope up from the riverside. They had little or no chance but even unwittingly they bought time for their employer's escape. Darius got clear but his army was ruined and his family were amongst the hefty haul of high status prisoners. While some of the mercenaries fought their way out of the trap, many more went down in its jaws. The great battle of Issus was over.

Darius kept to his chariot for as long as the ground allowed, then ditched the vehicle, together with his personal belongings, and jumped onto a fast horse. Only darkness brought an end to the chase. According to the main biographers, Plutarch, Arrian and Curtius, the toll of Persian dead exceeded a 100,000, ten per cent of those being from the elite cavalry and three senior officers, all of whom had survived the first battle, perished in this one. These figures, once again, are suspiciously high. Curtius tells us Alexander lost 450 soldiers with ten times as many wounded. That sounds more plausible.

And to the victors, the spoils. The Macedonians' haul was pretty impressive and many a weary phalangite would have cause to be glad he had joined up. Plutarch tells us Darius had parked much of his heavier baggage up in Damascus (Parmenion was sent off to grab this) and, by his standards, was travelling light. Still, there was more than enough loot to go around. Darius' tent, now Alexander's, was a marvel, 'glamping' in the grand style. The huge pavilions were crammed with gold and silver service, servants at the ready. Alexander made use of the Persian king's mobile ablutions suite, washing off the sweat and gore of victory in the luxurious pool of the defeated, a delicious irony. The place reeked of rare balms and exotic perfumes, with a sumptuous dining space adjoining. 'He turned to his companions and remarked "so this is what it is to be a king"' (Plutarch: 21). Vast wealth and unlimited power are powerful narcotics; the liberator of the Greeks was perhaps coming to see himself, just a shadow at present, as an oriental despot.

While at dinner in the king's tent he found out he had netted Darius' mother, wife (who was also his sister) and two daughters. This was a real bonus, a chance to cement the victory.

Darius has earned opprobrium from western commentators by fleeing the field. He would have been a fool to stay once his flank was turned and he was personally at risk. Capture or death would have been fatal to his cause, to the empire. One defeat,

The family of Darius captured by Alexander. (Charles le Brun, Wikimedia Commons, US Public Domain)

however resounding, did not need to be the end of the war as long as the king lived and was free to raise fresh armies. He also knew Alexander would treat his royal captives well, not on humanitarian grounds (he could be as cruel and vindictive as any tyrant) but on the grounds of policy. Such high-ranking prisoners were invaluable bargaining chips.

As it was, Plutarch waxes lyrical over his hero's chivalry. The Persian women were imposingly regal and, in the case of Darius' queen and her daughters, Plutarch insists, absolute stunners. The Greeks had captured Darius' getaway chariot and kingly bow; his family assumed this meant he was dead. Alexander reassured them, saw to their comfort, ensured they had their servants and gear available and made sure they would not be troubled by rampant, licentious soldiery. He was taking good care of his myth.

This is when the confusion between Stateira and Barsine arises. The legend is that Alexander now found himself a girlfriend in Asia. Memnon of Rhodes had left an attractive widow, the seductive Barsine, of good family, well-educated and refined, captured after the fight when Damascus was taken:

These qualities made Alexander the more willing – he was encouraged by Parmenion, so Aristobulus tells us – to form an attachment to a woman of such beauty and noble lineage. As for the other prisoners, when Alexander saw their handsome and stately appearance, he took no more notice of them than to say jokingly, 'these Persian women are a torment for our eyes'. He was determined to make such a show of his chastity and self-control as to eclipse the beauty of their appearance, and so he passed them by as if they had been so many lifeless images cut out of stone. (Plutarch: 21)

The real Barsine was the daughter of a Persian father, Artabazus, satrap of Hellespontine Phrygia and a Greek mother. She was indeed the wife of Memnon of Rhodes. After his death, so the story goes, she and her children were sent by her brother-in-law to Darius as hostages. She is said to have fallen into the hands of Alexander, by whom it is alleged that she became the mother of Heracles. On Alexander's death in 323 BC a claim to the throne on this boy's behalf was urged (unsuccessfully). From a comparison of the accounts of Diodorus and Justin, it appears that he was brought up at Pergamum under his mother's care and that both were murdered in 309 BC.

Alexander allowed Darius' queen to undertake proper funeral rites for the vast pile of Persian dead (or at least those of rank) while his own battle casualties were given a splendid send-off. He distributed honours among those who had done especially well. Nicanor was made up to provincial governor for Cilicia and others likewise promoted. As a gesture of largesse he let the citizens of Soli forego the 50 talents they owed. He could afford to – he had got 3,000 as part of the haul from Darius' pay chest.

The conqueror then got a taste of Persia. He sits amidst the looted splendour of the east; even Achilles never had it so good. He has dreamt of this, focused his whole being on it and left the shadow of his father's achievement far, far back. Alexander of Macedon has finally arrived; the world is at his feet. Everything in his life has been preparation for this al fresco dining, eating off his enemy's gold plate, attended by his servants, quaffing his vintages. If this is the Ruler of the World's idea of camping, what must his house be like?

Alexander has brought this whole scenario into being and here, for the first time perhaps, he begins to see how it must be from now on. Issus is truly a game-changer. Darius is not finished but he is on the ropes, without much real prospect of a comeback. But that means Alexander himself must morph, from conqueror into ruler. He must learn that it is one thing to win a kingdom, quite another to hang onto it.

Plutarch digresses at this point to remind us of Alexander's virtues. Plutarch's king is Shakespeare's Henry V, the heroic ideal, dedicated solely to his craft, utterly subservient to his ambition. He angrily rejects overtures that he should choose a couple of pretty boys, or even eat comfort food. He is dedicated to the Spartan ideal of manly vigour, attained through constant hardship and puritanical self-denial. Plutarch stresses that he was not much of a drinker (an idea at odds with other evidence) and that he lingered over the round rather than quaffing it ready for the next:

> By Jove, I am not covetous for gold,/Nor care I who doth feed upon my cost;/It yearns me not if men my garments wear;/Such outward things dwell not in my desires:/But if it be a sin to covet honour,/I am the most offending soul alive. (Shakespeare: *Henry V*: Act 4, scene III)

Meanwhile submissions came in thick and fast. The ruler of Cyprus threw in the towel without a fight as did most of the great cities of Phoenicia – the exception being Tyre. This hard-won success must, if far less spectacular than any of his battles, rank as one of Alexander's great military achievements, arguably the most deadly siege since Troy. Once Cyprus fell then his conquest of the Levant and most of Asia Minor was complete. Perhaps the most glittering pearl in the imperial diadem now awaited him – Egypt. Fountain of civilisation, enigmatic, fertile, wealthy, the Nile Valley was a tremendous prize. A conqueror of nations had not really arrived till they had taken Egypt.

There was no battle. The Achaemenid governor struck his colours without a blow. Egypt was as ancient to Alexander as he is to us and the Persians were irrelevant. They had been in control for not much more than a century since Cambyses invasion and the Egyptians had broken away for a long period before being corralled again. The yoke had only been refastened a dozen years before Alexander's arrival. His triumphal progress was characterised by a couple of key outcomes: the foundation of Alexandria and his visit to the ancient oracle at Siwah. Arrian credits the king with choosing the site for the city which would bear his name:

> He was at once struck by the excellence of the site, and convinced that if a city were built upon it, it would prosper. Such was his enthusiasm that he could not wait to begin the work; he himself designed the general layout of the new town …. (Arrian: 3)

Plutarch tells us Alexander gleaned his ideas for the city from a dream. The settlement quickly swelled into a major city, in its own way perhaps the greatest foundation of the ancient world, only narrowly surpassed by Rome herself, a centre for trade, industry, the arts and learning.

One legend insists that the foot-print of the new centre was marked out using barley-grains (possibly an established practice) but that birds swooped down to eat up the seeds. This was interpreted favourably as an omen that settlers would flock here to grow prosperous. Hugh Bowden[1] expresses some doubts about this. He points out that Memphis remained the administrative capital for some time. Alexander's Egyptian tour took place in autumn 332 BC. It may, in fact, have been Ptolemy, who seized this great prize after the hero's death. Certainly he is the man who encouraged the growth of Alexandria. Probably it does not much matter; Alexander himself has got the credit, as he certainly intended!

Siwah Oasis would become familiar to a future generation of desert warriors, the fabled British Eighth Army, jousting in the long pendulum of the war in North Africa with the equally legendary Erwin Rommel and his Deutsche Afrika Korps. For Alexander it was the home of the Oracle of Amun. Just getting there was never an easy journey: '… when plains covered with deep sand appeared, it was as if they were entering a vast sea and their eyes looked

---

1 See *Alexander the Great – A Very Short Introduction* (Oxford; Oxford University Press 2014), pp. 56–67.

vainly for land' (Curtius Rufus: 4.11). After a tough crossing the Macedonians reached the great oasis. Siwah is in fact one of the most remote, around 50 miles long and a quarter of that in width.

At the Temple, the incumbent priests (who knew a bit about how to impress VIPs) addressed their visitor as the son of Zeus (Plutarch) or Jupiter (Curtius Rufus). Alexander asked if he was destined to rule over the whole world and they dutifully replied yes, as you would probably expect them to. He also asked if all his father's killers had been punished (you might wonder if he already knew the answer to that one?). Again, the priests provided suitable reassurance. Curtius Rufus for one thinks Alexander's adopting the title 'Jupiter's Son' was blinging it up a bit much but these things mattered. We might think this consultation was just pure theatre, modern rulers would probably rely on Twitter but, unlike most tweets, this had a good chance of being believed in a more credulous age. Moreover, it helped legitimise Alexander's new and additional role as de facto pharaoh.

He was crowned in Memphis, becoming pharaoh in reality. The classical writers do not tell us too much about this. Alexander understood that he had to appear to these people as their legitimate ruler, not as some foreign parvenu. He had branded himself as a liberator, not just another conqueror; the necessary rituals were an important part of the show. Alexander knew he could not hold down the territories he had acquired through fear alone, he needed to be welcomed. He knew he would have to march eastwards into the heart of the Persian Empire and seek out Darius for a final reckoning, so he needed the hinterland behind to stay quiet. And, if anyone did have doubts, the smoking stumps of once mighty Tyre were a handy reminder.

Alexander was victorious, his possessions already far greater than any previous European ruler. But the next march, into the interior, would test him even more. Here he was in the enemy's back yard, an enemy who could still draw down huge reserves from his boundless continent. He, Alexander, would be more extended than ever, with Darius fighting on interior lines. What the Macedonians now possessed was a full treasure chest and the resources of Asia Minor and indeed of Queen Nile herself to facilitate this next, crucial bound.

Having returned with his forces to the Levant, Alexander received a letter from Darius himself offering a deal. He would cough up 10,000 talents, cede all lands west of the Euphrates and give one of his daughters as a wife. Plutarch says Parmenion thought this was a pretty good deal. 'If I was Alexander I'd accept'. 'If I was Parmenion so would I', his chief quipped. Alexander had not come to barter. Darius could just give himself up or suffer the consequences and those consequences were getting ready to march.

Darius had ordered a general muster at Babylon, stripping the provinces of fighting men, building even greater numbers than before. But this was not a numbers game, many of the men who came in lacked weapons or training and the satraps were being sluggish. Darius must have felt the ground moving beneath his feet. Curtius Rufus tells us he was upgrading his heavier cavalry with horse armour and better weapons, building up his horse herds to increase the size of his mounted units. One innovation, and he knew only too well how much he needed new ideas, was the use of scythed chariots. He had 200 of these vehicles constructed.

This vast shambling beast marched out from Babylon to fight, spilling over the fertile plain, those two great mothering rivers Tigris (on the right) and Euphrates (the left). Once over the fast-flowing Tigris, Darius' scouts reported the Macedonians were also advancing, so he sent his cavalry commander Satropates on with a thousand fast horsemen to be his eyes and ears. An infantry division of six times as many led by Mazaeus formed a screen covering the river crossing and a commando charged with a scorched earth policy. Wasting the ground ahead of his army was intended to hamstring the Greeks while he could continue to rely on interior lines.

By now the Persians were at Arbela which Darius hoped to use as a forward base. Curtius Rufus tells us it took five full days to get his army over the River Lycus, from where he advanced 'eighty stades' (say 15 kilometres) further to the next wet gap, the Boumelas (now the Kazir), close to Gaugamela ('House of the Camel', according to ancient legend). Here he found a grand flat space, ideal for his tactical needs. He had learnt the hard way at Issus not to restrict his numbers and that these could only work for him if allowed to deploy properly.

Scythed chariots had been around in the east for a while, though they had never really caught on in the west. Curtius Rufus gives us a pretty good technical description: 'from the end of the chariot pole projected iron tipped spears, and to the cross-beam on each side they had fixed three sword blades. Between the wheel spokes a number of sarissas projected outwards, and then scythes were fixed to the wheel-rims some directed upwards and others pointing down to the ground, their purpose being to cut down anything in the way of the galloping horses ...' (Curtius Rufus: 4.5); cutting-edge technology you could say.

This terrain was spot on, wide, open, devoid of cover and with a long view. Just how many men he could field is open to debate. Curtius Rufus suggests an army twice as big as the last and that implies over a million men, so vast a muster that Alexander's scouts struggled to describe the numbers. Even if we do what is wisest with such estimates and drop a decimal point, 100,000 is still a very large army. Still, if we consider that Darius had some breathing space while Alexander travelled to Egypt and, based centrally at Babylon, could draw in contingents from just about everywhere, then so huge a force is by no means impossible and with shortened supply lines, he could feed and water them.

Alexander was not daunted. Eleven days later he crossed the Euphrates, sending the cavalry over first to cover the phalanx. Mazaeus, Darius' local commander, did not dare to attack. Alexander did, he fully intended to fight as soon as possible. This was sound strategy; if he had to chase Darius over the bare interior, the land wasted ahead of him, it would be infinitely more difficult, his numbers suffering the inevitable attrition of long marches in enemy territory. Having skirted the fringes of Armenia he finally reached the mighty Tigris. All around the land still smoked, not a crop unburnt or a single animal left behind. Darius, he knew, was somewhere up ahead behind the river barrier.

He allowed several days for his men to rest then took them across the Tigris. This was a major feat. The river was deep and swift, swirling eddies and treacherous currents with a rocky floor that gave no grip. Heavily laden infantry, carrying their weapons and gear, especially the unwieldy sarissa, were going to struggle. If the crossing was contested it could easily turn into a bloodbath. Great rolling clouds of dense smoke billowed from burning fields on the far side and Alexander feared an ambush. He sent light horsemen ahead to scout the fords. The enemy was not there. Mazaeus had seriously missed a trick.

Heavy cavalry followed but even mounted men struggled in fast, shifting water that came up to the horses' necks in places. The name Tigris, Curtius Rufus informs us, means 'arrow' in Persian. The Greeks now found out why. Even when safer crossing places had been identified it was a tremendous struggle to get the men over. Most had their packs stuffed with loot and were not about to let their haul go, no matter what. Alexander used his cavalry as breakwaters, shielding the struggling phalangites as they stumbled across, slipping on smooth worn stones. In places there was near panic and it was impossible for officers' commands to be heard. Had the Persians struck at the hopelessly exposed column it might have been their salvation, but Mazaeus lacked the nerve and the moment past, exhausted bedraggled men stumbled up the far bank and caught their breath.

Alexander's boldness and nerve which, if he had failed, would have been classed as recklessness, paid off again; this formidable wet gap was crossed. Too little and too late, Mazaeus sent 1,000 cavalry forward. Alexander riposted with his own allied light cavalry under Ariston and saw the Persians off. In the scrap Ariston levelled a lance at the senior commander Satropates, spiked him, then chased the wounded man down to finish him off with decapitation. 'The head he brought back and, to loud applause, laid before the king's feet' (Curtius Rufus 4.25); all in all, not a bad morning's work.

The army made camp and the troops were allowed to recover from their ordeal but then there was a lunar eclipse, not a good omen and the men's fears boiled over into near mutiny. They had come too far, the gods had abandoned them, even the rivers were against them, time surely to turn back. Alexander countered smartly; he brought out his tame Egyptian seers, the spin doctors of their day and they produced a helpful interpretation; the Greeks were the sun and the Persians the moon. When the sun eclipsed the moon, this was bad news for the easterners, victory was assured. It worked. The men stopped grousing and resumed their march in good order.

Alexander's army was moving forward with the Tigris on their right and high ground to their left. And now it seemed Darius was coming. The Greek columns shuffled out into line and went on in battle order. They need not have bothered, these Persian forces were only stragglers, soon cut off and cut up. In his keenness to be out of the way Mazaeus had been slacking, much of his effort to deny the Greeks any supply had been half-hearted and quantities of grain with other provisions were brought in. Besides, the scorched earth policy gave added encouragement for the Macedonians to keep moving.

Darius' army was only about 30 kilometres away and the king had tried to bribe some or any of Alexander's men into assassinating him. He thought he might read the letter out aloud to show his men what confidence he had in them. Parmenion pointed out that it only needed one to be swayed and Alexander would be at risk. For once, he listened to his old general's advice.

Now Curtius tell us this was when Darius' captive queen died, he claims from exhaustion and despair, not in childbirth. Alexander halted the march to ensure the dead woman's funeral rites were properly attended to, befitting someone of her exalted status. Her widower, on hearing the news, was thrown into paroxysms of grief, thinking the Greeks had just done her in out of malice. When a trusted eunuch told him the truth, how Alexander had done his best for her and Darius' other family and had seen she got a proper send-off, he was moved with respect for his enemy's chivalry.

As a last-ditch effort to avoid battle Darius sent another deputation to offer terms. He upped the bung to 30,000 talents, offered Alexander everything west of the Euphrates, a marriage alliance and his son Ochus as a hostage. The ambassadors did point out that oversize empires were impossible to hold together. Alexander listened and then debated. Parmenion was for taking the deal, even the king himself might have drawn breath. It was a good offer. He would still have an empire, bigger than any Greek ruler before, a full pay chest, valuable alliances and, presumably, a happy army. He pointed out that 'giving' him everything west of the Euphrates was not much of a gift as he already possessed it. Ultimately he could not just stop. Alexander was a prisoner in his own myth and he had to see it through. It was time for the biggest of big battles, as a later tyrant in the same region would remark, 'the mother of all battles'.

CHAPTER 6

ROXANNE

One must live as if it would be forever, and as if one might die each moment; always both at once.

Mary Renault: *The Persian Boy*

A battle for the domination of the world. It reads like a sound bite but that was what Alexander's army was contending for, even the most raw recruit humping his *puissant* sarissa would have got that. And these were not raw recruits. They had come a very long way together and most were veterans of at least one major battle. Some might have fought at Chaeronaea, the Granicus, Issus and Tyre, following their young general. These men had never tasted defeat.

Veterans of the war in the Western Desert (1940–1943), often describe their experience in terms of the ocean, the vast limitless, baking horizons, seemingly like great shimmering seas. The barren plain of Gaugamela may have seemed like that to the Greeks as they advanced across it.

They marched in the late summer's dark. It was Alexander's intention to fight at dawn but they stopped roughly three and a half miles (5.6 kilometres) from the enemy. Having halted the army, he went ahead with scouts to recconoitre Darius' position. As he returned, Parmenion, normally ultra-cautious, suggested a night attack. Alexander vetoed this as too risky. It was 31 September 331 BC and Alexander marshalled his troops in what was, by

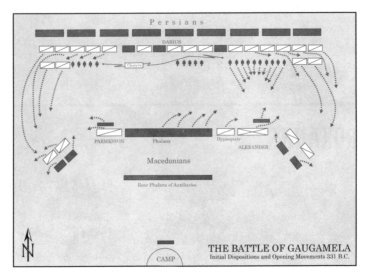

The following labels appear within the diagram:

Persians

DARIUS

Chariots

PARMENION   Phalanx   Hypaspists   ALEXANDER

Macedonians

Rear Phalanx of Auxiliaries

CAMP

THE BATTLE OF GAUGAMELA
Initial Dispositions and Opening Movements 331 B.C.

The battle of Gaugamela, 331 BC. (Chloe Rodham)

now, a familiar deployment. Plutarch tells us he was so supremely confident of winning, he overslept and brigade commanders just issued their own orders for the day: 'Then, as time was pressing, Parmenion entered Alexander's tent, stood by his couch and called him two or three times by name; when he had roused him, he asked how he could possibly sleep as if he were already victorious, instead of being about to fight the greatest battle of his life?' (Plutarch: 32). Alexander replied he had already won; he had brought Darius to bay. They would not have to chase after him across endless plains. It is probably apocryphal but a nicely constructed building block in the hero-myth.

On his right he placed the Companions, then the *hyspaspists* bolstered by three battalions of phalangites. The cavalry from the right comprised Cleitus' squadron, then those of Glaucias, Aristo, Sopolis, Heraclides, Demetrius, Meleager and Hegelochus with Philotas as overall divisional commander. Nicanor was in charge of the hoplites with the phalangites drawn up in brigades, Coenus to the right, then Perdiccas, Meleager, Polysperchon, Simmias and Craterus (who was overall commander). To the left of them would stand the allied cavalry, Greeks and Thessalians. Parmenion would, as ever, be Alexander's presiding general on the left flank.

Alexander knew that, on this level plain, the enemy's greater numbers raised the fear both flanks could be enveloped in a double pincer if Darius could manage it. So, he attached two flying columns, mobile wings, on both left and right. These columns were made up of light and heavy infantry, missile troops with light cavalry. These flanking brigades were deployed in echelon, slanted towards the rear, able to move rapidly either to foil an envelopment or create one. In front of the right-wing cavalry, he posted a line of archers and skirmishers as picquets to take on the Persian scythed chariots, in modern terms an anti-tank screen.

Alexander had approximately 40,000 infantry and 7,000 cavalry.[1] His deployment was both rigid and flexible with sufficient 'punch' in just about any direction to see off threats and exploit opportunities. As a final reserve and baggage guard he placed his Thracian infantry in front of the camp. This flexibility, as Curtius Rufus reminds us, would prove decisive.

Ahead of the Macedonians stretched the length of the Persian line, the full weight of a great empire at bay. The fearsome chariots deployed in front on both flanks. Not even veterans of Issus had seen anything like this. It was as though the whole of Asia had united in its own defence, a staggering display. Between the chariot units Darius had stationed his heavy Scythian cavalry. In the second line, from left to right, were his Bactrian horsemen, then two further mounted brigades with more infantry on his far right. Behind them, in their usual position, the great heaving mass of foot-soldiers, a united nations of Persia, divvied up according to location.

Plutarch tells us more, that Alexander treated his men to a rousing oration, proper Agincourt style. It is an unlikely tale, of course, as only a handful could have heard him. It is said the seer Aristander pointed out an eagle hovering overhead. As the great bird of prey

---

1 For a first-class account of the battle which neatly combines the classical sources, we have relied on Colonel J. F. C. ('Boney') Fuller's version, in his *Decisive Battles of the Western World,* John Terraine (ed.) (London; Paladin 1970), pp. 87–114.

Plutarch is quite light on detail when it comes to recording the actual fighting but he gives us a fine description of Alexander's **kit**. He probably got this originally from Callisthenes and it certainly fits the Homeric mould. The king had on a fine tunic from Sicily belted and worn under a padded linen arming jacket. The latter was presumably of Persian origin as he tells us it was lifted from the loot at Issus. His polished steel helmet, made by a Greek armourer, was worn with a matching section of neck protection – a blinged-up gorget. We don't know if his sword was leaf bladed or the Kukri-like kopis, probably the latter for a cavalry man but it had been a gift from a client-king, beautifully crafted and wonderfully light in the hand. He used this in preference to the lance. That is a hero for you, *get as up close and personal as possible*. His horseman's cloak came from Rhodes, fit for the god of war. Before contact he mounted old Bucephalus – past his prime but still game.

obligingly swooped towards the enemy line it must have seemed that this was surely a great omen of victory to come? Curtius Rufus goes into more detail; Alexander's address sounds rather more like a carefully constructed manifesto added in after the event. Battlefield oratory tends to be pithy and direct.

Take the words of Seutonius Paulinus, for example. The later, Roman biographer Tacitus, who gets his core narrative almost directly from the horse's mouth, his future father-in-law (Julius Agricola) was the general's aide, recorded how Seutonius prepared his vastly outnumbered army for the big battle against Queen Boudicca of the Iceni. Seutonius was very much a soldier's soldier. He did not waste words or prettify the task ahead:

Disregard the clamours and empty threats of the natives! In their ranks, there are more women than fighting men. Unwarlike, unarmed, when they see the arms and courage of the conquerors who have routed them so often, they will break immediately. Even when a force contains many divisions, few among them win the battles – what special glory for your small numbers to win the renown of a whole army! Just keep in close order. Throw your javelins, and then carry on: use shield bosses to fell them, swords to kill them …. (Tacitus, *On Imperial Rome* translated by M. Grant [Middlesex, Penguin 1956] XIV, pp. 14–65)

Darius must have wondered just what Alexander was intending: the Greeks did not come straight at him but advanced in an oblique line (see map on p. 108), right wing leading and aiming for the Persian left. Darius was obliged to conform or risk being outflanked as the Macedonians were angling away from the flat ground he had had swept level and bare. He sent in his 'heavies' to disrupt the move and compel Alexander to halt his advance. The king deployed his allied skirmish line but they were no match for heavy cavalry and were swiftly pushed aside in some disorder. Alexander tried to bolster them by throwing cavalry squadrons forward. Darius now committed the bulk of his mounted forces. The Macedonians had not encountered these well-mounted and armoured Scythians before: they crashed into the Companions, breaking through.

It must have been a hugely confused, swirling melee of horses and riders. For once the elite Companions found themselves facing an enemy better equipped than they and suffered heavily, great clouds of dust and steam shrouding the boiling mass. Alexander had to commit more and more squadrons to soak up the impetus of the enemy's charge. Clausewitz tells us all about the diminishing power of any offensive; he could have been writing about this situation. The great tide was at last halted, then turned back, the situation restored, and Alexander's right wing held. That crisis had passed but there were more to come. Curtius Rufus puts this recovery down to Alexander's personal example, twinned with outstanding leadership – there is no reason to doubt him on this.

Seeing his cavalry possibly gaining ground, Darius next launched his scythed chariots against the phalanx to pin Alexander's infantry. The Macedonian light infantry and skirmishers came into their own, sending volleys of javelins and a storm of arrows. But Darius had sent his juggernauts in at full tilt, the momentum careered them into the Greek infantry. Curtius Rufus tells us, they carved up a few ranks with their dreadful scythes and projecting spears. Though the light infantry recoiled, the chariots had been slowed and could not penetrate the phalanx: their sarissas stopped the chariots dead.

A detail of Darius from the Alexander mosaic (Pompeii). (Meister der Alexanderschlacht, Wikimedia Commons)

Gaps were deliberately opened to let the charging vehicles through then phalangites stabbed at the horses and brought them down, closing in to butcher their occupants. These vaunted chariots were something of a one-shot weapon. They had broken in but could not break out or maneouvre to inflict more damage. Nor could they retreat, swallowed up in the great jaws of the phalanx. Very few charioteers would have survived:

> Horses and charioteers fell in huge numbers, covering the battlefield. The charioteers could not control the terrified animals which, frequently tossing their necks, had not only thrown off their yokes but also overturned the chariots, and wounded horses were trying to drag along dead ones, unable to stay in one place in

their panic and yet too weak to go forward. Even so a few chariots escaped to the back line, inflicting a pitiful death on those they encountered. The ground was littered with the severed limbs of soldiers and, as there was no pain while the wounds were still warm, the men did not in fact drop their weapons, despite the mutilation and weakness, until they dropped dead from loss of blood. (Curtius Rufus: 4.16/17)

As the cavalry shook themselves out on his right and recovered both breath and order, Alexander sent two units to outflank the Persian horsemen trying to get around him. Then he led his whole brigade of Companions, formed as a striking wedge, for the gap in Darius' line his charge had created, supported by the four right-handed battalions from the phalanx. Darius himself was the target and the sight of so much personal attention again seems to have unnerved the Great King whose own left-wing cavalry, now on the defensive, were wavering. They broke and ran. So did Darius, covered as Plutarch tells us by his aristocratic bodyguard, most of whom were killed. The dead piles were growing around Darius thick and fast, his chariot horses got mired in corpses and he was forced, for a second time, to get onto a fast horse and gallop for his life.

This battle was not over though. As Alexander led his right wing forwards, his left, echeloned back behind, struggled to conform and a significant gap opened. More of Darius' cavalry galloped forward to exploit the hole and storm the Macedonian camp. Ostensibly their aim was to rescue noble hostages (Alexander had captured Darius' family at the battle of Issus) but chances for looting may have crossed their minds. Plutarch insists this was a careful manoeuvre ordered by Mazaeus. Macedonian discipline and training averted catastrophe as the phalangites smartly faced rear and advanced against the backs of these Persian cavalry, now sandwiched between them and the Thessalians. More horsemen swirled around Parmenion's exposed flank to complete his encirclement. It was almost as though two separate battles were being fought at once.

At one point the camp seemed lost. Alexander had sent a testy message to Parmenion telling him not to mind about the baggage, the loss could only be temporary. Nonetheless, it was unsettling for the Macedonians to think the enemy was in possession of their

Mosaic floor showing Alexander fighting Darius at Issus. (Unknown, Wikimedia Commons, US Public Domain)

stores (and accumulated plunder), even as mere squatters. The general had sent a galloper to Alexander begging for assistance. Plutarch is hard on the ageing officer, either he was past his sell-by date or just truculent and irritated by Alexander's youthful boldness, dash and, of course, success. Having said that, Alexander as commanding officer had allowed the dangerous junction to become unhinged.

So well trained were the Macedonian cavalry that Alexander, like Cromwell so very much later at Naseby, could trumpet the recall and they veered away from the satisfying pursuit of their broken enemies to reform and ride to the infantry's relief. Thumping into the flanks of the encircling clouds of Persian cavalry, they gave Parmenion's phalangites a much-needed breather. These Persians fought hard and stubbornly, shoved back yard by bloodied yard till a renewed push by the phalanx finally saw them off. Arrian records just how heavy and hard this fighting was: 'Conventional cavalry tactics – maneuvering, javelin-throwing – were forgotten; it was every man for himself, struggling to break through as if in that alone lay his hope of life. Desperately and without quarter, blows were given and received, each man fighting for mere survival without any further thought of victory or defeat …' (Arrian: 3.15). Around 60 of the companions died in this melee many others, including Hephaestion, were wounded.

No rest for the victors, they rode and marched after their beaten enemy all that long day, as far as the Persian base camp at Arbela. Darius again got clear but he had just lost what had been left of his empire. Curtius Rufus tells us 40,000 Persians had died (more realistic than Arrian's boast of 300,000), for the loss of 300 Macedonians. By dusk Alexander was indeed master of the world. Very few young men can have ever experienced that emotion which Alexander was now enjoying. This was a perfect triumph, Darius could never raise another army, he had run away once too often. Alexander showered his companions and his allies with honours and rewards; he let the Greek city states off any obligations; they were free citizens in a wider commonwealth. He could afford largesse; the wealth he had just acquired was beyond calculation.

Curtius Rufus maintained that Darius, whilst down, was not out – not just yet anyway. He had got back to his base at Arbela and held a conference of surviving officers. He was planning to regroup in the far corners of his empire, keeping only light forces with him. Let the Greeks take the big cities and be diverted with loot; this would buy him breathing space to rekindle the fight. In the circumstances this was bold talk; it is impossible to know how many believed him.

Within days Babylon, that fabled city of wonder, cradle of civilisations, saw the Greeks march in: Mazaeus himself handing over the keys and surrendering. This was a very rich prize indeed and the Macedonians wandered like tourists, awed by the famous mud-brick walls cemented with bitumen and the surviving extent of the great hanging gardens. The classical authors did not really approve of Babylon, far too opulent, reeking of decadence, her women far too easy in their ways, 'the moral corruption there is unparalleled,' Curtius prudishly reminds us. Apparently the ladies used to progressively remove clothing as dinner progressed (Curtius Rufus: 5.38). The hard-bitten Greek veterans, blood and dust of battle still clinging, must have been bewildered as well as stunned.

Alexander received reinforcements from the draft back home: 6,000 infantry, 500 cavalry with several thousand allied and mercenary troops, mounted and dismounted. It was not all sightseeing and relaxation. Alexander reorganised his cavalry units, regardless of race and origin. This was when he introduced a new brigadier level rank of *chiliarch,* officers chosen on merit through rigorous competition.

Then on to Susa, one of the greatest cities in the whole empire, nestling on the lower slopes of the Zagros Mountains and about 160 miles (250 kilometres) east of the Tigris; here his pay chest received a further boost with another 50,000 talents[2] worth of bullion being secured. Both Diodorus and Curtius inform us that Alexander inspected the sprawling imperial palace, finally penetrating to the throne room where he sat himself on Darius' vacant throne, a fine symbolic gesture, except being that much shorter, his feet dangled embarrassingly.

One of his equerries dashed over with a handy low table as an impromptu footstool. Seeing this one of the Persian eunuchs let out a wail, this had been Darius' eating table. Alexander seems to have been put out and wanted the table taken back but Philotas persuaded him to keep his boots on it, an acknowledgement of his supremacy. More recent commentators such as Hugh Bowden have suggested that Alexander was in fact enacting some form of coronation/succession ritual, parts of a broader hearts and minds programme. This stands to reason; Alexander understood the value of symbols and the use of drama to reinforce his myth.

Alexander next moved on to Pasagardae, Cyrus' ancient capital (located near today's Shiraz) and lifted a further haul of 120,000 talents worth of the shiny stuff. Before him stood the heartland of ancient Persia. It was mid-December when the army left Susa. Soon the fertile plain, temperate even in this late season was behind them, higher ground and looming mountains lay ahead. The hill-men, semi-autonomous highlanders, had been in the habit of 'taxing'

2 A talent weighed in at 75 lbs (33 kilograms). In today's money, with gold at around £30 a gram, a single talent would be worth around £982,000, so the Susa haul would amount to £54 million.

those who passed through. But Alexander was not about to play that game. The accounts are bit confused: but he seems to have stormed their pass in a lightning attack and soon had survivors begging for mercy. He was initially unwilling to accede but the locals managed to persuade Darius' mother to act as an intermediary and gain clemency. He stripped them of their flocks and baggage animals, leaving them near destitute but at least alive.

As the march resumed he sent Parmenion with most of the supplies and heavy infantry to take a more circuitous but easier route towards Persepolis. Alexander planned to lead the Companions and light infantry by the more direct, if seriously precipitous, route. And a very difficult road it proved to be. The narrow track wound through dense woodlands up 7,000 feet (2,134 metres) to the head of the pass. These were the Persian Gates, a narrow defile with what looked like a rampart of solid rock blocking the path. A defenders' dream; and it was defended. Perhaps as many as 40,000 Persians were ready, catapults loaded. The Macedonian vanguard ended up like fish in a barrel; rocks, sling-shot, spears, arrows, the lot, rained down on them. Alexander hurriedly withdrew the survivors to regroup. He had two choices; have another go or find another route? Alexander favoured the direct approach (as you might expect); beat the enemy here and the road to Persepolis would be open.

Like the Spartans, all those years before, the Persians were sold out by a local shepherd who knew of an outflanking path. It was risky but Alexander had to try. He left troops behind in the camp to keep the fires burning and provide a distraction while he led a force of chosen men up the wild and narrow sheep track. It was a long, hard slog in driving snow, five miles up to the head of the Bolsoru Pass. Here he sent four units of heavy Companion infantry to secure the ground beyond and towards the city. Alexander then led the light infantry and skirmishers on a further wild scramble to engage the enemy holding the road. They brushed aside the Persian outposts and then took on the rest while the bulk of the Macedonian forces came on from their camping ground to kick in the front door. It was a classic pincer and Alexander's boldness paid off again. The defenders were badly cut up, the rest did a runner and the road was clear.

Bas relief on the stair of the ruined palace at Persopolis. (Leon Petrosyan, Wikimedia Commons, CC-BY-SA 3.0)

Ancient **Persepolis**, the spiritual heart of the Achaemenid empire stood about 60 kilometres north-east of present day Shiraz in Iran. Construction may have been begun by Cyrus the Great around 515 BC but most of the early building seems to have been commissioned by Darius I. The programme was continued by his son and successor Xerxes and maintained for decades after that. A whole mighty range of vast, monumental civic and religious structures were completed though it is not likely, given its remote and alpine location, that the place was ever a functioning administrative capital as were Susa, Babylon and Ecbatana. It was essentially ceremonial, probably used at New Year (still an important festival in the region) and as a diplomatic and imperial palace complex to wow VIPs. Prior to Alexander's conquest of the place, the Greeks had never really heard of it. Whether the destruction was a systematic humbling and humiliation or just incendiary looting that got out of hand is uncertain though it is not something today's Persians have forgotten.

The ruins of Persepolis today. (MatthiasKabel, Wikimedia Commons, CC BY-SA 3.0)

Now he finally occupied the ceremonial capital of Persepolis, the very heart of Darius' empire. Here he heard of Antipater's great victory over Sparta and that the threat to the home front had been crushed. The gods indeed were smiling. Rather less so than on the city itself; this was immolated. Persian rulers had a habit of stamping their authority through acts of wanton destruction so Alexander's vandalism wasn't anything new, though classical writers saw this as a frolic rather than policy. At a drink-fuelled dinner in Persepolis Alexander was apparently persuaded by the Athenian hetaera, Thais, to set fire to the whole place as retribution for the torching of her native city by Xerxes. Some archaeological evidence supports this, surviving scorch marks would suggest that furnishings and flammable contents were piled up as bonfires to get a decent blaze going.

It may be true. Obviously Alexander's original *casus belli* was revenge for the destruction wrought on Greece by the Persians. Whether the appeal to destroy Persepolis came from Thais or from more sober approaches cannot be known. We know Alexander could be utterly ruthless, just ask the Thebans, and to have inflicted damage on important centres such as Babylon or Susa made no sense. Military conquest has to be backed by economic success, vandalising a populous entrepot was totally counter-productive. Persepolis had great symbolic significance but no commercial aspect so, if anywhere had to be trashed it was the most obvious target.

The death of Darius. Engraving by Bernhard Rode, 1769–70. (James Steakley, Wikimedia Commons, CC-PD-Mark)

In that winter of 330 BC, Alexander marched on to Ecbatana (today's Hamadan) and netted another fabulous hoard of 180,000 talents. Fugitive Darius was still on the run and running hard, Macedonian hounds close on his trail. His former subordinate Bessus beat Alexander to it and apparently 'arrested' the Persian king. After a furious chase covering nearly 400 miles in just over ten days, Alexander's men arrived just after the Persian turncoats had completed a bloody assassination.

Plutarch tells us that when Alexander's cavalry finally overran Darius' column, they found nothing but confusion and the man who had been king of the world pin-cushioned with the javelins of his own men. One of the Greeks brought the dying man a cup of water and Darius went out well, asking the man to thank Alexander for the care of his family. When Alexander found the king dead, he covered the corpse with his own cloak and saw his remains decently disposed of. Bessus, when Alexander caught up with him, got no thanks for his treachery, he was lashed to bent trees and ceremoniously ripped apart.

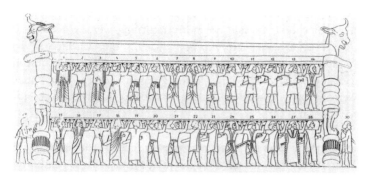

Archaeological drawing of the tomb of Darius the Great at Naqsh-e Rustam. (Alborzagros, Wikimedia Commons, CC-BY-SA 3.0)

This was the final piece of the imperial and dynastic jigsaw. Alexander was undisputed king of kings; *capo di tutti capi*. The first great strategic objective he had set himself as he crossed the Hellespont, the conquest of Persia was complete, the most extensive empire in history, wealthiest and most powerful, had been completely defeated and effectively subjugated. Now, he faced a completely fresh challenge. Conquest without assimilation, without enduring control is pointless. He had to consolidate, he had to persuade this whole great slew of ethnicities, faiths and regions to accept him as high king.

In general, the classical writers see Alexander's adoption of local custom as a symptom of irrevocable moral decline, the cancer of deified status eating away, corrupting his democratic heritage. This is too simplistic. As Hugh Bowden points out, the Macedonian kings were by no means unfamiliar with Persian regal custom. If he was to win those hearts and minds he needed to appear as the natural, indeed legitimate successor to Darius III. Wearing the robes of a Persian monarch as opposed to the armour of the oppressor is just part of this but an important part.

Our classical writers were appalled by the suggestion that Alexander required inferiors to prostrate themselves, a form of abasement which was anathema to free born Greeks. But Alexander was no Macbeth, sliding into the pit of tyranny, increasingly paranoid and vengeful: 'I am in blood stepped in so far, that should I wade no more, returning were as tedious as go o'er ...' (Shakespeare: *Macbeth*, Act 3, scene IV). He was the founder of what was effectively a new world order; a fusion of east and west which, while it could remind the easterners they were no longer top dogs, could not afford to rub their noses in it for too long.

Alexander indeed began to look east; way, way beyond any region the Greeks had ever penetrated (other than in legend). He had both to finish the detail of conquest by stamping his authority on the eastern satraps and bring some measure of security to a wooly, ill-defined pale. This was a fabled journey, a trip to the roof of the world. He marched to the shores of the Caspian, that wide inland ocean, then plunged on eastwards to Herat. Here he founded a city that would bear his name (the time for modesty was long past). Then, down the valley of Helmand, which a far more recent generation of soldiers will have cause to remember. He swung north-west to found another Alexandria at Ghazni and yet another near Kabul.

Next spring, 329 BC, he led his army up the steep Khawak Pass to the high ceiling of the Hindu Kush (*Caucasus Indicus* to the Greeks). This was truly the stuff of dreams, even mythical Hercules and Dionysius had not got this far. This dazzling range is a 500-mile (800-kilometre) canopy near to the present Afghan-Pakistan border, linking central Afghanistan to northern Pakistan, dividing the valley of the Amu Darya (ancient *Oxus*) to the north, from the Indus River valley to the south. It is capped by a range of soaring peaks, the highest being Tirich Mir or Terichmir at 25,289 feet (7,708 metres). Near its north-eastern tip, the Hindu Kush buttresses the Pamir Mountains where the current borders of China, Pakistan and Afghanistan meet.

Beyond the Oxus River and Bactria lay the endless rolling steppe, inhabited by wild Scythians. Alexander took his *blitzkrieg* forwards, pushing a fortified frontier line to the banks of the Jaxartes (now the Syr Daria). Here he set up a chain of outposts, centred on Alexandria Eschate (now Khojend). He bound the Bactrians and Scythians to him, marrying King Oxyartes'

The necropolis at Naqsh-e Rustam in Iran. (Roozbeh Taassob, Wikimedia Commons)

daughter Roxanne. Now whether this was a love match or just canny political nous, who can say, perhaps a dash of both. She was a beauty, very young at this stage and destined to produce his legitimate heir.

It was at this time he had, or may have had, his fabled encounter with the Queen of the Amazons. When in Scythia, he had overawed the king who had offered his daughter in marriage – this seems to be the origin of the tale. Whether or not these feisty female warriors ever existed has been controversial but, as Plutarch tellingly points out, when Alexander himself writes to Antipater chronicling his recent experiences, he makes no mention of Amazons. Something, you would assume, that no true son of Achilles would ever be likely to omit.

He now had India in his sights. Many writers see this as evidence that Alexander was driven to go on and on till he reached the ends of the world; that the demons of his ambition recognised no limits. Partially, at least, this must be true. Yet one of the problems with a conquering army is that you have to give your men fresh lands to aim for. Armies fight, it is what they are for. The Macedonians were paid wages but loot was the real prize. So far they had done very well indeed out of this campaign. However they might grouse tramping up the long reaches of the pass, probably blind to the wild, exotic glories of the Hindu Kush, they would be cheered by the prospect of fresh lands to plunder. Plus it kept them occupied. Once the war is done, once the fighting is over, an army has to adjust; garrison life is not the same and bored soldiery can become dangerous.

It was not just the rank and file who might get restless. Plutarch and the other writers, frothing about Alexander's descent into the deadly coils of oriental despotism, got a bit worried about his track record for politically motivated murders of friends on his own side. They saw this as evidence of degenerative paranoia brought on by the base seductions of the east. Was Alexander increasingly paranoid? Probably but that, as they say, does not mean nobody is out to get you. He came from an extended line of dysfunctional princes; internecine bloodletting was a long-held family custom. His father, after all, had been murdered, probably with the connivance of his mother who had gone on to see off her younger rival and infant child. It was a very rough neighbourhood.

It was in the closing months of 330 BC that a new conspiracy came to light. Philotas, old Parmenion's son, had been one of Alexander's closest companions and a very successful subordinate in his own right. Whether he was himself an active player or whether he simply knew a plot was afoot and stood back is not clear. Either way it did not matter; he was arrested, tried and condemned. Parmenion was also done away with at the same time. This was shocking even in such a brutally robust society.

Arrian dismisses the affair quite readily but Curtius goes into far more detail, a real courtroom drama which may or may not have been crafted for the benefit of a Roman audience familiar with the trials of Cicero and with an appetite for lawyer's rhetoric. Plutarch tells us Philotas had become bloated with ambition and corrupted by luxury. Even Parmenion had cause to get angry at his son's boastfulness. Like any good tale of fatal vanity Philotas unburdened himself to a concubine, a captive taken in war. He claimed to her (full of drink), that he and his father were the real architects of Alexander's victories. Craterus, who had set the whole thing up, reported the foolish claims to Alexander.

It was at this point that a half-baked cabal of conspirators were beginning to plot. Philotas came to hear of this but vacillated to the extent that his informers began to doubt him and took their tale straight to the king. This was probably the last in a set of nails for Philotas' coffin. He was clearly unpopular and Alexander was now inclined to listen to wagging tongues. Once he moved it was with the speed of a cobra, listening behind a curtain as his old friend and boyhood companion was tortured. It was all up for Philotas and for his father too. Here even Plutarch shows little empathy. Parmenion had been a loyal servant to father and son; he had already sacrificed two sons on the altar of Alexander's ambition. It was a particularly nasty irony that his brilliant career should end in such an arbitrary manner. This was as much as anything *pour encourager les autres*. Paranoia is contagious; the wagging tongues may just have paused to consider who might be next. Antipater, back in Macedonia guarding the home fires, must have felt very exposed. Success and long service were no talismans for longevity.

And next there was Cleitus. Of all Alexander's misdeeds this is the most infamous. There had been various portents that all was not well. While Alexander was at dinner with his officers, including Cleitus, whom we may remember is credited with saving his life at the Granicus battle, someone began to sing ribald songs having a go at certain Macedonians who had been beaten by the Persians. The rest were none too happy but the king didn't seem bothered. All had been drinking and none more heavily than Cleitus.

Alexander announced a reorganisation of commands. Specifically, Cleitus was given orders to take 16,000 of the defeated Greek mercenaries who formerly fought for the Persian king north to fight the steppe nomads in Central Asia.

Cleitus knew that would make him a forgotten man, no longer a member of Alexander's entourage. Furious at the thought of commanding what he saw as second-rate soldiers, fighting nomads in the middle of nowhere, he spoke his mind. To make matters worse, when Alexander arrogantly boasted that his accomplishments were far greater than that of his father, Philip II, Cleitus responded by saying that Alexander was not the legitimate king of the Macedonians, and that all of his achievements were due to his father. Alexander called for his guards, but they did not want to intervene in a quarrel between friends.

Alexander was offended and high words passed between the two men. A typical drink-fuelled quarrel between two old friends who should have known better. But maybe Cleitus was articulating the resentment some of his officers were feeling at Alexander's going native and this was what irked the king so much. It became a free for all with the older fellows trying to calm everyone down and failing, Cleitus' anger became vituperative. Alexander became so enraged he hurled an apple at his friend then looked for his sword which someone wisely had removed. He was so angry he got ready to call out the guard while Cleitus' friends dragged him out. Fatally, he was not done, perhaps the perfect riposte came to him outside and he had to make his way back in to deliver it. He sneaked in by another door and started a tirade. Whereupon Alexander lost control completely, grabbed a spear from one of the guards and spitted his old friend who died on the spot. That was the end of the party. Alexander was filled with remorse but dead is dead.

Three years later, in 327 BC, another dark plot surfaced. A clique from among his royal pages, all of whom had access to the king, plotted his murder. Alexander cheated the assassin's knife again and the conspirators were unmasked and dealt with. One who fell into the net was Callisthenes himself, Alexander's own court historian. He may have been done to death or possibly died whilst in custody of natural causes. Alexander might have spotted the chance to have a clearout after the unsuccessful plot; it provided an ideal opportunity for filtering out any who had expressed opposition to Alexander's increasingly despotic regime. As others had discovered, he could be as fickle and vindictive as any tyrant. Increasingly so as he came to seem invincible. Plus it is possible that the physical toll of his campaigns was making him more aware that he was physically vulnerable. Even Achilles had been killed in the end and he was practically an immortal: Alexander was not.

Plutarch tells us of the catalogue of wounds he had amassed. His father had died with a long tally of old wounds, his son seemed likely to do the same. In Scythia Alexander had been hit by an arrow in the upper calf. This had splintered his shin-bone which had required surgery to get the fragments out. He had also been hit in the neck (presumably by a sling-shot) which had affected his vision for a noticeable period. None of these diminished his energy though, had he lived into middle age, he would have probably paid a lasting price. But Alexander of Macedon was not done yet.

CHAPTER 7

RETREAT

Made it Ma! Top of the world!

James Cagney: *White Heat* (1949)

Elephants are big, they are very big, and decked out for war they are downright frightening. Alexander was sufficiently impressed that his victory coins, struck after the Hydaspes battle in 326 BC, or at least one of them, figure a lone cavalryman attacking a war elephant, manned by a driver (mahout) and a warrior who is busy chucking javelins at the horseman. This may well represent Alexander squaring up to his enemy in the battle – the local ruler, Porus. The reverse of this medallion shows the conqueror, in full war gear with thunderbolt and a wreath of winged victory. The battle of the Hydaspes would be Alexander's fourth big fight in the east and tactically the most challenging, another brilliant win.

Having crossed the lofty spine of the Hindu Kush, Alexander had penetrated into the northern rim of the great Indus basin (now Pakistan). It is likely (according to Herodotus) that Darius I had campaigned in this region, extending his sway and consolidating his eastern marches. Arrian for one tells us that some Indian troops had stood with Darius III's Bactrians at Gaugamela and had even brought some war elephants with them, though these had, or so it seems, played little or no part in the fight. No Greek armies had ever come this far, that is for sure and Alexander stormed a seemingly

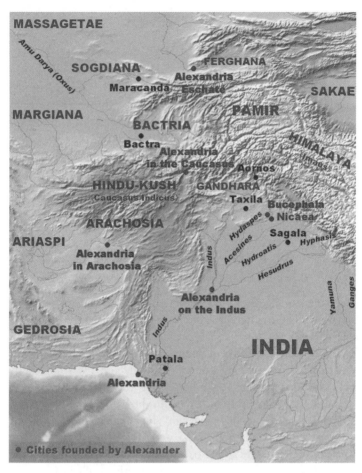

Map showing the location of Pir Sar. (World Imaging, Wikimedia Commons)

secure fortress, the Rock of Aornus which was said to have been too big a job even for Heracles.

The location is disputed but Pir Sar, a spur or plateau above bends in the upper flow of the Indus is the current favourite guess (see map above). This fortified hilltop was well supplied, virtually inaccessible and commanded the valley floor below. As long as it remained in hostile hands it was a major threat to the narrow umbilical of Alexander's attenuated supply line. Robin Lane Fox views Alexander's last great siege as justifying his reputation as the greatest besieging general in history. Certainly going one better than Hercules was bound to impress.

Alexander almost certainly recruited local guides from neighbouring tribes who had surrendered. Ptolemy was charged with doing a detailed reconnaissance. He identified and took a projecting spur on the west side and fortified the ground with stockade and ditch. The defenders pretty soon picked up on this – the Macedonians invested two days of difficult skirmish and manoeuvre in clawing their way up the sheltering ravines around the fortress. The north elevation, from a besieger's point of view, looked the most promising and Alexander brought up his artillery only to be foiled by a deep, intervening ravine. This had to be bridged and then an artillery platform thrown up. A solid day's work brought the catapults 50 metres closer.

It was hard and immensely challenging, the ravine, even though it was now bridged, fell away sharply into nothingness, so the viable frontage was very narrow. At the end of day three the Greeks could grasp a toehold on the massif via a col (the lowest point on a mountain ridge between two peaks) leading up from an outlying ridge. Undismayed, the defenders rolled large boulders down the slopes, pushing the Macedonians back. Cunningly, Alexander let himself appear disheartened as the enemy drumbeats echoed their sense of victory (Indian armies preferred drums to trumpets we are told). Then he took the place by a lightning assault, himself leading the scaling party. The locals fled or died where they stood. Alexander erected altars to Athena Nike to mark this very significant tactical achievement.[1]

Aside from the military significance, this was sending a pretty clear message to local princes – there is nowhere to run. Alexander moved on to the city of Nysa which was associated with that other

---

1 Sir Marc Aurel Stein (1862–1943) a Hungarian-born British archaeologist and explorer, very active in the Great Game, identified the site during one of his four major expeditions in the early 20th century. His report on Aornus is written up in his 1929 *On Alexander's Track to the Indus: Personal Narrative of Explorations on the North-West Frontier of India* (London; Macmillan & Co. Reprint: New York, Benjamin Blom 1972).

War elephants, Persia, 4th century AD. (Alieh Saadatpour, Wikimedia Commons, CC-BY-2.0)

great journeying hero Dionysius. The latter was said to have been raised there by rain nymphs (the *Hyades*), his signature plant, ivy, was found growing there and yet seen nowhere else in the vicinity. Now a quartet of rivers flow down into the mighty Indus, spilling down from the Olympian reaches of the Himalayas, the Hydaspes (Jhelum), Acesines (Chenab), Hyaraotes (Ravi) and Hyphasis (Beas). A broad sweep of territory between these waterways was held by a motley crew of rival warlords. Alexander made no effort to interfere with local arrangements; rather he acknowledged all who submitted as satraps. Taxiles, an important chieftain who controlled ground between the Indus and the Hydaspes, was the first to bend his knee. His neighbour Porus, whose lands lay to the east of the Hydaspes, was less amenable. He preferred to make a fight of it and a fight he would have.

Porus commanded a force of up to 30,000 warriors, 4,000 cavalry, 300 chariots and as many as 100 war elephants. His main strike force were the elephants. These were the Indian variety, their tusks encased in brass, with a two-man crew; the mahout up front

These **war elephants** (*elephantry*) were not an innovation. Ancient sources such as the Rigveda (1200–850 BC) mention elephants being used for transport and haulage but not at that point for war. By the 4th century BC, however, there is talk of war elephants and their use was widespread enough to have influenced the Achaemenid kings. Darius had a small elephant corps at Gaugamela, but these either were not deployed or their deployment was impaired as they seem to have had no impact on the fighting. At the Hydaspes the Macedonians opened lanes to let the rampaging beasts through but they did plenty of damage with their armoured tusks and powerful trunks. Mahouts carried poisoned stakes in case the animal ran wild but so many of the drivers were killed by Greek missiles that the elephants ended up creating as much havoc among their own side. Alexander would subsequently have been aware his next opponents, the formidable Nanda Empire (Northern India from Bengal to the Punjab), had several thousand. On his return to Babylon, Alexander formed his own Greek elephant corps under the command of an *elephantarch*.

on the animal's neck and a warrior mounted behind with a quiver full of bamboo javelins. Both carried shields for protection. His cavalry were mainly light as opposed to heavies and infantry units were primarily formed of archers, shooting metre long arrows from bamboo longbows (1.8 metres). Spearmen carried hide shields: they had little or no body armour but their back up weapon was a long (1.12 metres), double-edged broadsword.

Alexander now marched towards the wet gap of the Hydaspes. The phalanx numbered around 14,000 with 3,000 hoplites, perhaps 10,000 Greek mercenaries and several thousand light infantry. He also had some 2,000 companion cavalry with a whole inventory of allied units, perhaps three times as many as the Companions in total. He came down onto the level through the Nandana Pass, the silver ribbon of the Hydaspes winding below, fields and paddies dotting the plain. The enemy had occupied the eastern bank of the wide river, a kilometre across, and dotted with a necklace of islands. Porus had blocked the main crossing points; his position was a strong one. He was not coming to meet the Macedonians; Alexander would have to cross the water before any contact.

Alexander needed to keep the enemy guessing. Having reached the river, he had reconnoitered the banks to identify possible crossing points and finally opted for a location shielded by Adama Island (which effectively screened his deployment). Moving under cover both of night and a drenching storm he left Craterus commanding a shadow garrison at the main ford, and Meleager with more men at a neck in the river before moving the main body to his chosen crossing point. He got the bulk of his cavalry strike force onto the island and then over to what he thought was the east bank. That turned out to be just another irritating islet – getting fully over started to become a tricky business at that point. Barges were bringing up the bulk of the infantry. Porus had been humbugged as the Duke of Wellington might have said. No easy matter though, the sight of the sheer mass of the enemy and the difficult river crossing rattled the Macedonians: 'The combination of the river and the enemy suddenly struck terror into hearts which were generally given to confidence and had often proved themselves in battle; for the Macedonians believed their unstable boats could neither be steered to the bank nor safely landed there' (Curtius Rufus: 8.13).

Alexander led the cavalry ahead as a vanguard and screen while Porus, recovering from his surprise, sent forward his own vanguard led by his son (or brother according to Curtius Rufus), with 4,000 cavalry and 100 chariots. Now these Indian vehicles were real battle wagons, each with a crew of six; two with shields to give cover, a brace of bowmen and a pair of drivers who could also double up as fighters at close quarters. The Indian forces were relying on these chariots but the monsoon had churned the ground so badly they quickly got bogged down. Alexander struck with his light and then heavier cavalry, realising Porus could not come up quickly enough to support his son/brother who, along with many others, was killed in the melee. Rider-less chariots were careening madly, others mired in the squelch. First blood to the Greeks but Porus got his main forces moving as both sides jostled for position.

Alexander kept his cavalry in hand, moving forward from the wreck of the Indian vanguard to screen the steady shaking out of the infantry line behind. Porus threw out a line of elephants with cavalry massed on his left flank, foot units mustered behind the ponderous pachyderms. Quite a sight and another novelty for the Greeks, this great line of those huge animals, with a mass of spears and banners behind, delivering a whistling rain of missiles as soon as the armies came within range. As usual Alexander formed his mounted regiments up on his right and attacked the Indian cavalry on that wing. Porus, deficient in cavalry at best, attempted to move reinforcements over from his far wing. Alexander detailed Coenus to ride around behind the phalanx (rather as he did at Issus), to create a pincer. Coenus was Parmenion's son-in-law but that had not stopped him being one Philotas' most vociferous accusers. He had proved himself on many occasions but he, better than anyone, knew that provided no guarantees.

Porus' cavalry could not cope and pelted back behind the line of elephants to regroup. Alexander sent in his skirmishers to harass horsemen and elephants; the cavalry bit back and tried to see them off, giving Alexander the chance to charge them again. The battle moved swiftly towards a denouement. Up came the phalanx, Greek cavalry on the right, driving off what was left of their mounted opponents. Arrows and javelins took out drivers and warriors. At this point, the elephants panicked and stampeded everywhere, no use to anyone. The phalanx opened ranks to let them blunder through. A fierce infantry fight boiled up before Porus' infantry crumbled beneath those inexorable sarissas, going down in droves. Even their bows were ineffective. Curtius Rufus tells us the draw-weight was such the stave needed to be grounded to manage the full draw. The very wet ground did not help.

Plutarch says this is how Alexander himself described the action in one of his dispatches home; another resounding victory. Despite the scale of his triumph, he was disposed to be magnanimous and Porus, after his surrender, was treated leniently and, once he had sworn loyalty, was left in peace. Plutarch tells us Porus was a giant of a man, over six foot three (1.9 metres), both brave and intelligent.

Curtius Rufus almost waxes lyrical, however condescendingly: 'Porus himself rode an elephant which towered above the other beasts. His armour, with its gold and silver inlay lent distinction to an unusually large physique. His physical strength was matched by his courage and he possessed as much acumen as could exist among savages' (Curtius Rufus: 8.13). Alexander was so impressed he even gave his vanquished enemy additional territories – Porus now controlled 15 tribes, 5,000 decent sized towns and more villages than you could count.

At this point Alexander lost an old friend. Aged around 30, old Bucephalus had ridden his last mile and died (probably of old age but possibly from wounds in the fight). His distraught owner founded a city, Bucephalia, in the faithful charger's memory. He did the same for a favourite hound so Plutarch informs us. Plutarch is also convinced that the battle of the Hydaspes, whilst a great victory, pretty much exhausted the Macedonians who had really had enough. Why not, they were thousands of miles east of their homes, beyond the furthest border of the Achaemenid Empire, further even than Heracles or Dionysius might have gone. The next wet gap was the Ganges, huge, wide and deeper than deep with heathen hordes beyond, numbers beyond counting swarming on the far bank. Enough was enough.

They would go no further. Alexander went into a right royal sulk, languishing and truculent in his tent. The army would not budge, this was no passing shower – it was a regular storm of protest. Even Alexander of Macedon could not go on without his army; he had reached the limit of empire, if not of his ambition. We do have to ask if his displayed agony was genuine dismay or pure theatre. Alexander was well aware that his two major priorities were to firstly secure the eastern frontier of his newly acquired empire and then secondly, to consolidate his grip on the rest. The legend of the Alexander whose vision of domain was boundless was a necessary element of his own personal brand. It had got him this far but he probably knew that this was far enough. And he needed keep things at home under control. He would have had dispatches from the interior telling of restlessness, corruption and plot, standard fare of the Achaemenid Empire.

Head of Hephaestion, c. *320 BC. (Unknown, Wikimedia Commons)*

It had certainly been his expressed intention to reach the Indian Ocean which, Greek mythology insisted, circled the globe. To exploit this ocean of dreams he had brought a corps of shipwrights in his train. They set to work, cutting down the abundant timber to build a fleet of galleys and barges, a significant achievement in itself. Once ready, elements of the army embarked and cruised down towards the mouth of the Indus. Alexander led the flotilla with his highly competent commodore Nearchus undertaking the navigation. Craterus marched the bulk of his forces on the bank, keeping pace.

This journey was a long way from a Greek *Wind in the Willows;* the populous settlements by the river sometimes had to be subdued by force. One tribe, the Malli, were notoriously independent minded. Alexander, as ever, led the storming party: 'After the defenders had been driven from the walls by volleys of missiles, he was the first to

The Susa weddings, late 19th-century engraving. (Tarawneh, Wikimedia Commons, US Public Domain)

scramble to the top of the wall by means of a scaling ladder. The ladder was smashed so that no more Macedonians could join him, and the barbarians began to gather inside along the bottom of the wall and to shoot at him from below …' (Plutarch. 61). This was not so good. Being Alexander, he leapt inside the walls rather than back out and landed on his feet covered by his shield. At first he pushed the opposition back as two of the Companions, Peucestas and Limnaeus, joined him. His armour took a pounding as he fought but one archer got lucky and at point blank range the arrow punched through his body armour piercing the ribcage. The fellow drew again to finish the job but Alexander, desperately wounded as he was, nailed him first.

The two heroic companions hurled themselves forward but Peucestas was wounded and Limnaeus killed. Alexander was taking hits left, right and centre, almost downed by a blow to the neck. Happily, more Macedonians fought their way in and rescued the king who had nearly lost consciousness. The arrow wound was serious and deeply embedded. First his surgeons had to sever the protruding shaft to lift off the battered breastplate then carefully cut out the head which was lodged firmly between the ribs. It was a very close shave and could easily have done for a lesser man. As it was he took a good while to recover and was undoubtedly, in the longer term, weakened by the wound. He was using up his nine lives and it took all of seven months to navigate the deep winding reaches of the mighty Indus.

In due course Craterus was sent back overland to Persia while Nearchus piloted his ships across the Indian Ocean and around the Persian Gulf. Alexander took the remaining soldiers back over the inhospitable Gedrosian Desert (the coastal regions of Baluchistan in modern Pakistan). This did not work out too well, the land was bare and inhospitable and the army suffered badly. Modern writers tend to think the classical sources grossly inflated the horrors of this march – Plutarch tells us three quarters of the army perished, plainly nonsense as he only had a fraction of his available forces with him. Some even think he was deliberately punishing the men for their earlier insubordination. More plausibly, he may have been emulating Cyrus the Great who also fared badly, showing that he, Alexander was superior.

> Here he endured terrible privations and lost great numbers of men, with the result that he did not bring back from India so much as a quarter of his fighting force. And yet his strength had once amounted to a 120,000 infantry and 15,000 cavalry [a wild over-estimate]. Some of his men died from disease, some of the scorching heat but most from sheer hunger …. (Plutarch: 66)

The whole crossing, Plutarch goes on to tell us, took 60 days. The episode of bacchanalian excess described in chapter 2 occurred after this rough march as the army made its way through Carmania (now the Kerman region).

It is easy to take a soap opera view of Alexander but he had demonstrated his capabilities many times. We should, in all his actions, look for the policy, the *realpolitik*. There is little real evidence he had sunk into the sybaritic and vicious ways attributed by the Greeks to Persian tyrants. His efforts to integrate better with his Persian subjects had clearly upset his Macedonian officers but they were soldiers; he had also to be a statesman. Simply to conquer Darius' empire was not enough. He had to show this vast caravanserai of disparate peoples that he was both a legitimate and worthy successor. He had to set the boundaries as the whole eastern flank of Achaemenid possessions was wide open. This cruise down the Indus and the march itself were largely exercises in flag waving. And, from a purely strategic point of view, to continue east towards the Ganges would have made sense if the army had agreed, leaving the whole wide plain of the Indus as defence in depth, a Pale in India.

Once clear of the desert wastes, the road to Pasargadae and Persopolis, then to Susa and Ecbatana and finally Babylon lay open. While still in Gedrosia Nearchus joined him again and he was enthused by the tales of the fleet's voyage. He began, Plutarch says, to think in terms of a grand circumnavigation of the African continent, sailing down the Euphrates, past the Arabian Peninsula, cruising from east to west and getting back into the Mediterranean through the Pillars of Hercules. A nice plan but he had more pressing matters to focus on. His absence had sparked a series of local risings and his provincial governors had been misbehaving, lining their own purses and stirring up resentment. Exploration would have to wait. News from home was no better, Olympias and his sister Cleopatra had fallen out with Antipater, trying to carve up the homeland between them.

It was time to put some stick about and he did. Nearchus would conduct an amphibious campaign against any malefactors in the coastal provinces while Alexander marched inland. Plutarch tells us he killed Oxyartes (not his father in law but the son of the satrap of Susiana), spitting him on a sarissa. When the man's father Abuletes proffered cash instead of the supplies he had been ordered to amass, he was gaoled. A Macedonian who had looted the tomb of Cyrus the Great was summarily executed; the new imperial justice was impartial, as indeed it needed to be. Not that it was all responsible government and good behavior. Plutarch tells us of an epic binge

Photo of a relief in the Hellenic War Museum showing Alexander being rescued. (Tilemahos Efthimiadis, Wikimedia Commons, CC-BY-SA 2.0)

where Alexander and other contestants tested their capacity for booze. The winner got a crown but the drink did for him and another 41 of the participants.

He now married Darius' daughter Stateira. Polygamy was common enough in both Macedon and Persia and such a marriage alliance further legitimised the conquest and demonstrated his intention to act as a bonafide ruler, not just a foreign oppressor. Numerous of the Companions were instructed to do the same at a mass wedding in Susa. Hephaestion was married to Stateira's sister Drypetis, cementing the links between the two men.

He next had to deal with another near mutiny of scarred Macedonian veterans who felt he was treating his new Persian recruits far better than they: his countrymen feared they be dumped and left destitute. After the usual show of recriminations and mutual foot-stamping, he ensured due provision was made for all the oldsters.

Then came disaster. Hephaestion caught a fever and, having ignored doctors' advice, quickly succumbed. This was a huge personal blow to Alexander; his friend/lover was no grizzled old soldier but a young man normally full of vigour. Plutarch tells us he had the unlucky physician crucified. Distracting himself with action, he marched against a troublesome nest of highland bandits, the Cossaeans (a rather vaguely known tribe from the Northern Zagros Mountains in Western Iran). He subdued them and wiped out the whole male population.

Towards the close of 324 BC Alexander moved on to Babylon, despite earnest warnings from Nearchus and others that the omens were far from favourable. He was sufficiently worried to pitch his tents outside the city walls where more dire predictions piled in thick and fast: 'a tame ass attacked the finest lion in his menagerie and kicked it to death', Plutarch warns (though you have to ask what kind of lion gets duffed up by a tetchy donkey). Worse, some bonkers imposter was found sitting on the imperial throne, clearly disturbed but Alexander played safe and had him killed anyway. But even this has echoes of ritual. The substitute fool was a feature of Persian regality, the shadow or proxy king, usually a convict or lunatic, set up to take on misfortunes that should otherwise have fallen on the real king and then got rid of.

Much of this seems to have been a manifestation of Alexander's own growing paranoia. Without new lands to conquer he had leisure to begin doubting all around him. Chief suspect was Antipater. Despite having proved a loyal and efficient regent who had kept the home front safe and seen off Memnon of Rhodes and the Spartans, he and his sons fell under suspicion. Cassander (who would be king) had just arrived in Babylon where he had to defend his father against the tide of whisperers. He made the mistake of voicing his contempt for those who abased themselves before Alexander. The king was incensed and treated him roughly, smacking his head off a stone pillar for his impudence. Plutarch is sure the humiliation and insult remained with Cassander for life: he later showed no clemency to Alexander's son by Roxanne or his bastard (possibly) from Barsine.

He had filled the palace with quacks and soothsayers obsessed with portents and the supernatural, 'a slave to his fears', Plutarch informs us. Was he really? We should be careful not to place undue weight on the classical sources here. This descent into rampant paranoia fitted the whole decline and fall device. Plutarch, Arrian, Curtius

Cassander with his brother Iolas were sons of the regent Antipater. Like Alexander, Cassander was educated by Aristotle, alongside Ptolemy, Hephaestion and others who formed the core of the hero-king's most intimate circle. There was also a distant blood kinship. We first hear of Cassander when he arrived in Babylon in 323 BC, sent by Antipater to fight his corner amongst the detractors. The reception he got clearly turned him against Alexander and that animosity persisted long after the king's death. Cassander went on to rebuild Thebes and showed nothing but disdain for the king's memory. When Antipater was on the way out in 319 BC, he did not nominate his own son as successor, possibly fearing his ambition. Cassander seized the regency anyway and canvassed support from the other Successors. He attacked his father's nominee Polyperchon and, after two years, assumed the regency by force. Of course, Alexander's half brother Philip III was nominally ruler at this time. Olympias was bidding for power in her own right and Cassander bottled her up for two years in besieged Pydna. Once in his power he killed her and then both Roxanne and her son and a royal bastard named Heracles (possibly Barsine's child). He married Alexander's half sister Thessalonike (the city is named after her), and saw off any challengers. It did not do him much good; he died of sickness in 297 BC and his putative dynasty failed to thrive.

Rufus et al are playing to an audience of their times and spinning a moral tale. The brave young man from the west, full of noble intent, is seduced by the shuddering vices of the east and has to suffer the consequences; Shakespeare would have loved it. We can see now that Alexander *had* in part to conform to Persian custom, he could not hope to consolidate his position otherwise. Plus, Eastern courts always attracted their fair measure of fakes and chancers.

Soon after, the history of Alexander of Macedon reached its climax. He fell ill with a fever which worsened day by day. He lingered for a week or so. The end came 'on the thirtieth day of the month Deasius'.[2] A comet had fallen. Alexander, the most proficient and successful soldier of the classical age (and most others), was dead

---

2 10 June 323 BC.

Farewell to Alexander by Karl Piloty. (Tarawneh, Wikimedia Commons, US Public Domain)

at 32. He had no son (Roxanne's baby was yet unborn) and had nominated no heir, nor even a regent. Gods do not die of fever so young. England's near equivalent, Henry V, would die at the same age, also of sickness and with disastrous long-term consequences. It is said Alexander predicted great sport at his funeral games and great sport there was. But not the kind you find in the arena.

The Macedonians recognised Roxanne (or rather her as-yet-unborn child) as legitimate successor. She nonetheless took the useful precaution of having Stateira and her sister murdered.

At the time nobody suggested Alexander had been assassinated; the conspiracy theories (and we do so love them) did not begin until five years later when someone 'fessed up. Olympias apparently had a number of individuals killed in response. Fingers were pointed at Antipater, perhaps the obvious choice. Had the regent in Macedon decided on a pre-emptive strike rather than wait for he and Cassander to become the next Philotas and Parmenion? Aristotle was said to have been the instigator.

Why Aristotle, his old mentor? The relationship between teacher and student had cooled and it may be Alexander began to have

Alexander's catafalque (19th-century depiction) based on Diodorus. (Tarawneh, Wikimedia Commons, US Public Domain)

doubts. Aristotle would be aware of how dangerous this might be and had the unfortunate example of Callisthenes to ponder. It's equally possible that accusations against Antipater were put up by his enemies during the subsequent power struggles.

On the balance of probabilities we should probably decide his death was down to natural causes. The injuries he had taken, particularly the chest wound sustained in the Punjab just the year before, must have weakened his constitution and he was a very heavy drinker. His own death paralleled that of Hephaestion and nobody then had shouted foul play. Though he seems to have lost the power of speech, sinking into a coma, a few days before he died the story circulated that, before he became incapable, his companions asked about the future, to whom would he will his kingdom? His reply was 'to the strongest'. True or not, that is the way it was bound to go.

CHAPTER 8

FUNERAL GAMES

*Why, man, he doth bestride the narrow world
Like a Colossus, and we petty men
Walk under his huge legs and peep about
To find ourselves dishonourable graves.*

Shakespeare: *Julius Caesar* Act 1: II

Alexander's funeral was indeed attended by great games, nothing however compared to the sport to be had over the succession. He had not nominated an heir, his son, if indeed it be a son by Roxanne, was yet unborn and the army had no candidate with the right credentials, experience or charisma. As there was no natural successor a whole legion of hopefuls stepped forward and the business quickly came to resemble the bloodier sort of Jacobean tragedy.

Perhaps the most dominant character was Perdiccas, one of the most able cavalry officers. He found himself up against an infantry general, Meleager, who wanted Alexander's older half brother Arrhidaeus to succeed. Despite being older, he appeared to be discounted as a potential ruler because, according to Plutarch, he suffered from severe learning difficulties. Alexander had kept him around, partly as a kind of mascot and, presumably, to keep him free of court intrigues. Perdiccas favoured Roxanne's unborn child who was indeed a boy – he would become Alexander IV. The deal eventually patched together was that half brother (now Philip III)

Bust of Ptolemy, 3rd century BC. (Marie-Lan Nguyen, Wikimedia Commons, CC-PD-Mark)

and infant son would rule jointly with Perdiccas as regent, the *éminence grise.* No sooner was this agreed than Perdiccas began bumping off his rivals starting with Meleager, his short-lived deputy.

Much good it did him. Perdiccas, despite the ruthless severity of his rule, fell out with too many people, leaving enemies in every quarter. He finally attacked Ptolemy in Egypt in 321 BC, made no headway and was assassinated by his disgruntled officers. In the meantime he had dismembered Alexander's vast, unwieldy inheritance and parceled out governorships or satrapies amongst various generals. Ptolemy had got the great plum of Egypt. Arrhidaeus, ruling as Philip III, never really exercised any actual control but did contrive to die in his bed of natural causes, an achievement in itself. Roxanne and her boy, both shielded by Olympias until her death in 316 BC, were then murdered.

No sooner was Alexander cold than the Greeks, true to their fissiparous tendencies, rebelled against Macedonian domination, a serious uprising which threatened the home front. The able Craterus, who was joint ruler of Macedon with Antipater, had to come back and get stuck in. He defeated the Athenians at the battle of Crannon in September 322 BC and the revolt failed.

Inevitably the satraps founded their own competing dynasties and a series of Successor Wars flared. The final and fourth Diadochi war ended with the battle of Ipsus in 301 BC. That really marks the end of Alexander's great empire. His conquests flared like a comet across the skies of history, then guttered and went out. The great adventure was over, mired in a squalid scrabble of petty rivalries and talentless greed. The classical age in many ways died with Alexander and the Successor Wars opened up the stage for a new and dynamic player.

Michael Grant has described the Roman army as a 'corporate force'.[1] It was. Rome possessed a standing army; the sword of the state, which from a tradition rooted in the hoplites of Greek city states, would grow and develop into the anvil of empire. Like his Greek predecessor the original legionary was a citizen, a man of property and position who could afford to turn out with his own kit. He had a personal stake in the survival and expansion of the state but he only expected to serve for the duration of hostilities. Essentially, he was a small farmer who went to war when called upon. Nonetheless, he was tough, resourceful and competent.

On 22 June 168 BC Aemilius Paullus brought three exhausting years of war with the rump of Alexander's Macedon to a successful denouement at the battle of Pydna in Greece when the legions utterly thrashed the mighty phalanx. Rome had finally arrived as a global superpower and Macedon had gone. Rome had previously tamed her rivals on the Italian Peninsula, won the long, bloody and costly wars with Carthage and was set to expand.

The phalanx disappeared into history but not for good. King Robert the Bruce, fighting for Scottish independence in 1314 at Bannockburn, made good use of massed spears, his hardy *schiltrons* which Alexander's phalangites might have recognised. They would

---

1 Michael Grant's *The History of Rome* (Faber and Faber 1986).

certainly have seen the Swiss pike formations which dominated European battlefields in the late 15th century as natural successors. The 'puissant' pike became a standard infantry arm throughout the long wars of the late 16th and 17th centuries, till finally displaced by the bayonet.

In the 14th century soldiers of the emergent Swiss cantons had employed halberds to great effect, winning significant victories at Mortgarten (1315) and Laupen (1339). Gradually, and partially in response to a defeat at Arbedo in 1422, the Swiss began to increase the ratio of pikes to halberds in their ranks.

This unstoppable mass of resolute points could smash through enemy formations like a steamroller; movement, mass and cohesion welded together into a formidable instrument of war. Swiss armies were characterised by relentless discipline, constant aggression and swelling confidence. Charles the Bold of Burgundy, that rash adventurer, confronted the Swiss in the 1470s and suffered a series of catastrophic defeats, at Grandson, Morat and finally, Nancy, where his last army was decimated and his own life forfeit. Since then the Swiss had turned war into a trade, selling their genius for wages, which, if not forthcoming, would produce immediate defection. These Swiss fought wars as an industry, not for glory. Even Machiavelli was impressed.

Alexander was a living legend and the lustre never faded; the sorry little wars of his successors just served to show the breadth of his genius. From the date of his death, he would be the benchmark for any conquering general. Caesar, Marlborough and Napoleon would judge themselves against his performance. Fundamentally, he changed history, not just that of Greece but of the world. A few generations earlier Xerxes had set out to conquer Greece. On paper the weight of his force and vast resources were unstoppable. The Three Hundred dented his coronet, their countrymen saw him off, Xenophon showed what might happen. Alexander made sure it did. From now on the west would move east and not the other way round. Iraq and Afghanistan are not the only manifestations of this.

One wonders what Alexander would have made of the Western-backed coalition which defeated Daesh in Iraq and Syria. The war was essentially asymmetric and once we had all woken up to the

A modern Afghan soldier in a fortification believed to have been built by Alexander. (U.S. Air Force photo, Staff Sgt. Manuel J. Martinez)

danger, pretty one-sided but the confidence and relative ease of the forces deployed is Alexander's legacy. He will be with us for a long time yet.

In the 19th century Alexander was popular in Britain, partly due to a combination of the classical revival, archaeology and an over-robust spirit of empire. He was touted as taking the ideal of Greek culture and conferring it on decadent Persians, barbarous Asiatic types and primitive tribesmen, a bit like Caesar in Gaul. That rose-tinted view has now been replaced by a more balanced view of empire, horror at the glorification of war and fetishisation of weapons. No doubt if he or his descendants were alive today, they would be called upon to apologise.

One of his early biographers, Arrian of Nicomedia, writing in the 2nd century AD, begins with an apology, 'why should he presume to write yet another history when so many have all been written.' Nonetheless his is one of the fullest extant accounts; his *Anabasis* is essentially a pretty detailed military history. Arrian writes nearly a century after Plutarch who was more concerned with understanding his subject, his charisma, drive and ambition. He clearly admires

Alexander but does not dodge the warts, his occasional cruelty; the booze-fuelled murder of Cleitus. It is thanks to Plutarch that we know pretty much what he looked like. The author drew on the work of Alexander's favourite sculptor Lysippus.

He remains as popular a topic as ever. Among modern writers, the most readable account is Robin Lane Fox (who acted as technical advisor to Oliver Stone in the making of the 2005 movie, sporting a blond wig himself and leading a cavalry charge at the age of 58!). Lane Fox read nearly 1,500 previous studies before embarking on this epic work. Both Paul Doherty and Paul Cartledge have written notable biographies. Doherty views his subject as a ruthless tyrant, a classical Stalin. Of course, you have to be aware that applying modern judgments to historical characters can make it harder to grasp the reality of their own time. You could say his was a reign of terror but most were, Greek and Macedonian domestic politics were a rough school, Pella was a pretty rough neighborhood. Alexander is best understood, if not necessarily approved of, by the standards of his own era.

Cartledge is more concerned with governance and administration than with war. He is brilliant in his specialised field though we do need to be aware that, for Alexander, war was governance! Alexander was indeed self-aggrandising, consciously modelling his public persona on heroes like Achilles (who was not a very nice man either). Yes he could be cruel, vindictive and marred by petty spite. The hero has feet of clay, like the rest of us, they generally do.

Alexander has also inspired fiction, perhaps the best-known trilogy of books are those by Mary Renault, *Fire from Heaven* (1969); *The Persian Boy* (1978) and *Funeral Games* (1981). These are marvelous reads, capturing an essence of time and place which is quite extraordinary. Renault, after serving as a nurse in World War II chose to live in South Africa with her partner, fearing the climate in England, which at that time disapproved of single-sex relationships. She does write extensively though with a very well-judged emphasis on Alexander's sexuality. Consequently she is rather light on battles. American author Stephen Pressfield's *Alexander: The Virtues of War*, is more of the Bernard Cornwell school. He gets straight into the nitty-gritty and he knows how to recount a battle.

Phalangite at ease. (By kind permission of John Conyard)

Richard Burton attempted to bring Alexander to life on screen in *Alexander the Great* (1956), written and directed by Robert Rossen and with Claire Bloom, Harry Andrews, Stanley Baker and Peter Cushing. It does not really work; actors run the risk of looking precious in the role: it is hard to communicate a combination of charisma with petulance.

Oliver Stone had another go in 2007. His *Alexander* was part written and directed by him, with Colin Farrell in the lead, Angelina Jolie, Val Kilmer and Anthony Hopkins. A true epic, it attempted to be historically accurate, though Farrell's Alexander was a rather cardboard character, preening and a bit prissy. The battle scenes were massive but confused. Reviews were at best mixed.

Hero or villain, or somewhere in between, Alexander is a colossus, one who shaped our history, ensuring the basis of our western civilisation would be the legacy of the Hellenic World and for that, if nothing else, our debt to him is inestimable.

SELECT BIBLIOGRAPHY

PRIMARY SOURCES

Arrian, Mensch, P., & Romm, J. S., *The Landmark Arrian: The Campaigns of Alexander* (Anabasis Alexandrous: a new translation (1st ed). New York; Pantheon Books 2010)

Diodorus of Sicily, translated and edited by C. Bradford Wells (Cambridge Mass; Loeb Classical Library, volume VIII 1963)

Plutarch, *The Age of Alexander,* translated by Ian Scott-Kilvert (London; Penguin Classics 1971)

Polybius, *The Histories,* translated by W.R. Paton in six volumes (Cambridge Mass.; Loeb Classical Library 1922–1927)

Quintus Curtius Rufus, *The History of Alexander* translated by C. Yardley (London; Penguin Classics 1984)

SECONDARY SOURCES

Adcock, F. E., *The Greek and Macedonian Art of War* (Berkeley; University of California Press 1957)

Allen, L., *The Persian Empire* (London; British Museum Press 2005)

Bosman, P. (ed.), *Alexander in Africa* (South Africa; University of South Africa Press 2014)

Bosworth, A. B., *Conquest & Empire; the Reign of Alexander the Great* (Cambridge; Cambridge University Press 1988)

Bosworth, A. B., *Alexander and the East: the Tragedy of Triumph* (Oxford; Oxford University Press 1998)

Briant, P., *Alexander the Great and his Empire, a Short Introduction* (Princeton; Princeton University Press 2010)

Cartledge, P., *Alexander the Great: The Hunt for a New Past* (London: Overlook Press 2004)

Carney, E., *Women and Monarchy in Macedonia* (Oklahoma; Oklahoma University Press 2000)

Connolly, P., *The Greek Armies* (London; Greenhill Press 1977)

Doherty, P., *Alexander the Great: The Death of a God* (London, Constable 2004)

Engels, D. W., *Alexander the Great and the Logistics of the Macedonian Army* (Berkeley, California; Univ. of California Press 2007)

Freeman, P., *Alexander the Great* (New York; Simon & Schuster 2010).

Hammond, N. G. L., *Alexander the Great, King, Commander and Statesman* (London; Chatto & Windus 1981)

Hammond, N. G. L., *The Macedonian State; Origins, Institutions & History* (Oxford; Oxford University Press 1989)

Hammond, N. G. L., *The Genius of Alexander the Great* (Carolina; University of Carolina Press 1997)

Hammond, N. G. L. & Wallbank, F. W., *A History of Macedonia* volume 3 (Oxford; Oxford University Press 1988)

Heckell, W. & Jones, R., *Macedonian Warrior* (Oxford; Osprey 'Warrior' Series 2006)

Heckel, W. & Tritle, L. A. (Eds.), *Alexander the Great; a New History* (Chichester, U.K; Malden, Mass: Wiley-Blackwell 2010)

Lane Fox, R., *Alexander the Great* (London; Penguin 2005)

Martin, T. R. & Blackwell, C. W., *Alexander the Great: The Story of an Ancient Life* (Cambridge; Cambridge University Press 2013)

Mosse, C., *Alexander: Destiny & Myth* (Baltimore; John Hopkins University Press 2004)

Peach, L. G., *Alexander the Great – an Adventure from History* (Ladybird Books; Wills & Hepworth 1963)

Randall, B., *Alexander the Great: Macedonian King and Conqueror* (New York; Rosen Publishing Group 2004)

Renault, M., *The Nature of Alexander* (London; Allen Lane 1975)

Romm, J. S., *Ghost on the Throne: The Death of Alexander the Great and the war for Crown and Empire* (New York; Alfred A. Knopf 2011)

Spencer, D., *The Roman Alexander: Reading a Cultural Myth* (Exeter; University of Exeter Press 2002)

Victor, D. H. (ed.), *Hoplites, the Classical Greek Battle Experience* (London; Routledge 1981)

ACKNOWLEDGEMENTS

You can blame Ladybird Books for this. Our school libraries had full sets and Alexander the Great was a particular favourite. The hero king was portrayed as a Macedonian Achilles, young, beautiful, dynamic, an Aryan ideal, his less attractive traits, a penchant for homicidal drink-fuelled rages and casual cruelties, were not highlighted. His sexuality was also airbrushed out. We had to wait for the excellent series of historical novels by the late Mary Renault for that insight. The gloriously kitsch sword-and-sandal films of the early sixties cemented the fascination. John spent time in the wonderful Shefton Collection (see below) secretly hidden away in Newcastle University. Few people seemed to find it – it was a 'lost' museum that allowed you to think you were in your own private collection.

Thanks are due to John Conyard, for kind permission to feature his superb photographs of re-created Macedonian and Greek warriors, to Adam Goldwater and Andrew Parkin of Tyne and Wear Archive & Museums ('TWAM'), to Ulfric Douglas for additional advice on weapons and equipment. Special thanks are also due to Ruth Sheppard, our editor at Casemate, on our seventh successful collaboration and, as ever to Chloe Rodham for the maps.

Any errors or omissions remain, as ever, the responsibility of the authors. Wherever possible we have attempted to identify owners of copyright material, if any omissions come to light then we should be pleased to hear from anyone concerned and will undertake to make the necessary changes/additions.

Rosie Serdiville & John Sadler,
Spring 2018

INDEX